PSYCHOLOGY RESEARCH PROGRESS

NEUROTICISM: THE PERSONALITY RISK FACTOR FOR STRESS AND IMPAIRED HEALTH AND WELL-BEING

PSYCHOLOGY RESEARCH PROGRESS

Additional books in this series can be found on Nova's website under the Series tab.

Additional E-books in this series can be found on Nova's website under the E-book tab.

PSYCHOLOGY RESEARCH PROGRESS

NEUROTICISM: THE PERSONALITY RISK FACTOR FOR STRESS AND IMPAIRED HEALTH AND WELL-BEING

SHARON GRANT

Nova Science Publishers, Inc.
New York

For permission to use material from this book please contact us:
Telephone 631-231-7269; Fax 631-231-8175
Web Site: http://www.novapublishers.com

LIBRARY OF CONGRESS CATALOGING-IN-PUBLICATION DATA

Grant, Sharon, Dr.
Neuroticism : the personality risk factor for stress and impaired health and well-being / Sharon Grant.
p. ; cm.
Includes bibliographical references and index.
ISBN 978-1-61668-689-5 (softcover)
1. Neuroticism. 2. Personality--Health aspects. 3. Sick--Psychology. 4. Stress (Psychology)--Risk factors. I. Title.
[DNLM: 1. Neurotic Disorders--complications. 2. Disease--psychology. 3. Personality. 4. Stress, Psychological--complications. WM 170 G763n 2010]
R726.5.G69 2010
616--dc22 2010013750

Published by Nova Science Publishers, Inc. † New York

CONTENTS

PREFACE

This book reviews the literature on the Big Five and physical and mental health, focussing on neuroticism as *the* personality risk factor for stress and impaired health and well-being. Although neuroticism is often associated with excessive or unfounded symptom and illness reporting, studies of objective health outcomes, such as longevity or mortality, have confirmed that the trait does indeed play a genuine role in objective health status. With regard to mental health, neuroticism is associated with a range of conditions, and recent work has linked the trait with DSM-IV personality disorders. In addition, neuroticism is a strong and consistent predictor of both subjective (hedonic) and psychological (eudaimonic) dimensions of well being. This book presents an overarching process model, describing the effect of neuroticism on various intermediate mechanisms that tie situational stressors to negative health and well-being outcomes. Evidence is reviewed linking neuroticism with stressor exposure and emotional reactivity, negative cognitive appraisal, maladaptive and ineffective coping, and risky health behavior. The combined/interactive effect of neuroticism and other traits on vulnerability is also considered. The book examines biological and psychological mechanisms underlying the toxic effect of neuroticism, and concludes with a discussion of possible intervention strategies.

Chapter 1

INTRODUCTION

The first section of this book provides a historical overview of the personality-illness relationship, including the role of psychological stress in mediating this relationship. Discussion of stress focuses on the Transactional Model of Stress and Coping, in which cognitive appraisal and coping mediate between potentially stressful events and the subsequent experience of stress, illness, and disease. The Five-Factor Model (FFM) of trait personality (extraversion, neuroticism, conscientiousness, agreeableness, openness) is then introduced as a powerful framework for understanding the role of personality in illness and disease.

The next section of the book identifies neuroticism as the personality risk factor for stress and impaired health and well-being. The section begins with a review of studies on the relationship between FFM personality and physical and mental health outcomes. Discussion of the relationship between personality and mental health focuses on DSM-IV personality disorders, a topic area which has generated considerable interest in recent years. The relationship between personality and well being in the general population is also discussed.

In the next book, explanatory mechanisms or mediating processes in the personality-illness relationship are examined. An overarching process model is presented which describes the effect of neuroticism on various intermediate mechanisms that tie situational stressors to health and well-being.

The book concludes with a summary and discussion of possible interventions to appease the detrimental impact of neuroticism. It is noted that future research should focus on the direct evaluation of explanatory mechanisms underlying the personality-illness relationship.

Chapter 2

The Personality-Illness Relationship: Where it Began

The idea of a relationship between personality and illness began in ancient Greek philosophy, with Hippocrates' notion of mind-body dualism (Brantley & Garrett, 1993). Hippocrates believed that four bodily humors provided the basis for personality: black bile, blood, phlegm, and yellow bile (Friedman & Booth-Kewley, 1987). The four humors were theorized to correspond with specific temperaments - melancholic (depressed), sanguine (optimistic), phlegmatic (apathetic), or choleric (angry) respectively – with a person's predominant humor determining his or her 'personality type' (Friedman & Booth-Kewley, 1987). Hippocrates' theory was later expanded by Galen, a second century physician who believed that humoral imbalance, an excess of any one humor, would give rise to illness and disease (Brantley & Garrett, 1993; Elliot & Sheldon, 1997; Friedman & Booth-Kewley, 1987; Michaels, Michaels, & Peterson, 1997). In contrast, a balance between the humors was thought to promote 'good humor' or well-being (Winter, 1996). However, with the emergence of Cartesian dualism interest in the personality-illness relationship declined and the area did not re-emerge as a legitimate field of scientific enquiry until much later (Brantley & Garrett, 1993).

Modern interest in the personality-illness relationship arose from Freudian psychology, in particular the psychodynamic treatment of hysterical paralysis (see Brantley & Garrett, 1993; Elliot & Sheldon, 1997; Friedman, 1990; Friedman & Booth-Kewley, 1987). Freud drew attention to the effect of unconscious conflict on physiological arousal and related symptoms (Emmons & King, 1988). The psychodynamic tradition gave birth to 'Specificity Theory', the notion that a given illness could be attributed to the influence of a specific trait or underlying conflict (Brantley & Garrett, 1993). By mid-century, there was considerable interest in the topic, which came to be known as 'psychosomatic medicine': the study of mental disturbance and organic disease (Friedman, 1990). Interest in Specificity Theory persevered throughout the 1950s and 1960s (Brantley & Garrett, 1993), however much of the research was methodologically questionable and the field eventually fell into disrepute (Friedman, 1990).

In the 1960s and 1970s, attention shifted to the relationship between quantifiable life events and illness (e.g., Holmes & Rahe, 1967), and psychological stress was introduced as a mediator of the personality-illness relationship (Brantley & Garrett, 1993; Lazarus, 1990). Since then, stress has become a pivotal context in which to examine personality and illness (see e.g., Wiebe & Smith, 1997).

While interest in the personality-illness relationship has fluctuated over time (Brantley & Garrett, 1993; Elliot & Sheldon, 1997; Suls & Rittenhouse, 1987), there is currently much interest in the topic (Korotkov & Hannah, 2004; Michaels et al., 1997; Wiebe & Smith, 1997), with considerable attention to the role of personality in the stress-illness relationship since the mid-1980s (Vollrath, 2001). Given the importance of stress and related concepts in the personality-illness literature, the stress-illness relationship will be discussed in some detail below.

Renewed interest in personality and health has been driven by the progression of health and personality psychology, and behavioral medicine more generally (Korotkov & Hannah, 2004; Suls & Rittenhouse, 1990). In recent years, studies linking personality to objective health outcomes, such as illness onset and longevity, have seen a resurgence of research in this area, with such studies dismissing longstanding criticism regarding the limited predictive validity of personality measures (Smith, 2006).

Chapter 3

STRESS AS A MEDIATOR OF THE PERSONALITY-ILLNESS RELATIONSHIP

The role of personality in stress and related health outcomes is recognized in epidemiology, physiology, sociology, and psychology, with each discipline adopting its own unique theoretical and/or methodological approach (Parkes, 1994). However, a central thesis, regardless of the discipline, is that susceptibility to stress-related illness and disease is not random but systematic; that is, a person may be more or less vulnerable or resilient on the basis of personality (Friedman, 1990).

Psychological models of stress vary, although most include a basic tri-level structure in which the effect of an antecedent variable or 'stressor' is altered by or filtered through moderating or mediating variables (e.g., cognitive appraisal, coping) to influence the outcome variable, 'strain' e.g., health (see Deary et al., 1996). Perhaps the most influential model to have emerged is Lazarus and Folkman's (1984) *Transactional Model of Stress and Coping*. Within this model, cognitive appraisal is theorized to mediate between the perception of a potentially stressful event and the subsequent experience of stress to influence the individual's psychological and physiological response to the event.

Cognitive appraisal can be defined as an individual's evaluation of the significance of a potentially stressful event for personal well-being, given his/her goals and needs (Kuppens, Van Mechelen, Smits, De Boeck, & Ceulemans, 2007). According to Lazarus and Folkman, the appraisal process is tri-phasic: (1) Primary Appraisal – assessment of the event's significance for personal well-being; (2) Secondary Appraisal – (a) assessment of what can be done about the event, given one's available resources and (b) subsequent initiation of a coping response; and (3) Reappraisal - re-assessment of the event, including whether a further coping response is required. It should be noted that cognitive appraisal is not necessarily conscious in this model (Siegall & Cummings, 1995).

Primary appraisal is subdivided into (1) 'irrelevant', (2) 'benign-positive' and (3) 'stressful' (Monroe & Kelley, 1997; Peacock & Wong, 1990), where the latter is thought to arise from the appraisal of (a) harm (possibility of damage/loss), (b) threat (possibility of future damage/loss), or (c) challenge (possibility of gain/growth and damage/loss) (Monroe & Kelley, 1997; Peacock & Wong, 1990; Tomaka, Blascovich, Kesley, & Leitten, 1993). Harm appraisal is 'post hoc' by definition, in that it does not occur until after the stressful event, while threat and challenge appraisal are 'a priori', occurring before or in anticipation of the stressor (Peacock & Wong, 1990; Tomaka et al., 1993). The appraisal of a situation as harmful, threatening, or challenging is associated with an alteration in the intensity of mood or affect, triggering a cycle of change in the person's psychological and physiological functioning (Cox & Ferguson, 1991; Dewe, Cox, & Ferguson, 1993; Siegall & Cummings, 1995). Challenge appraisal may fluctuate between potential growth/gain and potential damage/loss, and can therefore oscillate between a state of positive and negative physiological arousal (Semmer, 1996).

While primary appraisal is concerned with assessment of the event's significance for personal well-being (Callan, Terry, & Schweitzer, 1994; Peacock & Wong, 1990), secondary appraisal is concerned with assessment of whether one can manage the event categorized as 'stressful' during primary appraisal (Cox & Ferguson, 1991; Hobfoll, 1988; Monroe & Kelley, 1997; Peacock & Wong, 1990). During secondary appraisal, the individual must assess available coping strategies or preferred coping styles in light of the situation at hand and select a coping response (Cox & Ferguson, 1991; Matheny, Aycock, Curlette, & Junker, 1993; Peacock & Wong, 1990). A coping response is not initiated unless the event is appraised as stressful in the first instance therefore coping is dependent on the outcome of primary and secondary appraisal (Dewe et al., 1993; Siegall & Cummings, 1995). It is during the coping phase that the individual is able to test the 'workability' of secondary appraisal (Payne, 1991).

The fact that coping is interwoven with cognitive appraisal as a key variable in the stimulus-response process is a defining characteristic of the *Transactional Model of Stress and Coping* (Dewe et al., 1993; Monroe & Kelley, 1997). Coping, any behavioral or cognitive attempt to control, reduce, or prevent distress in the presence of internal or external demand (Folkman &

Lazarus, 1980; Lazarus, 1990), is thought to influence physiological arousal via its impact on (a) the intensity or duration of the stressor and/or (b) the likelihood that the stressor will recur or be appraised as stressful in the future (Wiebe & Smith, 1997). Although the central purpose of coping is to reduce tension and restore equilibrium through stressor reduction, coping may be adaptive or maladaptive (Parkes, 1994).

Stress is thought to arise from (a) the appraisal of an event as harmful, threatening, or challenging, and (b) the appraisal that an adequate or appropriate coping response is unavailable (Cohen, Kamarck, Mermelstein, 1983; Cohen & Edwards, 1989). The stressor is manageable to the extent that the individual's perceived coping resources (secondary appraisal) are appraised as high in relation to the perceived threat (primary appraisal) associated with the event (Bouchard, 2003). At a general level, stress is hypothesized to contribute to illness and disease through deregulation of (a) the autonomic nervous system (e.g., cardiovascular and neuroendocrine activity) and (b) immune system functioning (Brantley & Garrett, 1993; Brown, 1993; Michaels et al., 1997; Siegrist, 1995; Wiebe & Smith, 1997).

Reappraisal is concerned with the individual's *subsequent* assessment of the stressful event. Information and experience gained from the initial person-environment transaction is used to re-evaluate the situation and assess whether a further coping response is required (Tomaka et al., 1993). If the event is appraised as irrelevant or benign at this point, then no further coping response is initiated. If on the other hand, the event is still appraised as stressful, there is a continuation of the cognitive appraisal-coping-reappraisal sequence.

To summarize, according to the Transactional Model of Stress and Coping, an individual's response to a potentially stressful event is a function of the perceptual inter-face between person and environment, as opposed to the quality or intensity of events per se (Cohen et al., 1983; Fleming, Baum, & Singer, 1984; Monroe & Kelley, 1997). With regard to strain, the causal mechanism is the individual's cognitively-mediated response (cognitive appraisal, coping) to the stressful event, the product of which is related to physiological arousal and subsequent vulnerability to stress-related illness and disease (Cohen et al., 1983).

Several of models theorize a central role for personality in this process. For example, personality may influence the likelihood that a person will experience a stressful event (stressor exposure), his/her assessment of that event (cognitive appraisal), the selection of more or less adaptive coping strategies (coping), the extent of his/her emotional or physiological reaction (reactivity), and the etiology and progression of stress-related illness and disease e.g., due to underlying pathology (Cohen & Edwards, 1989; Friedman, 1990; Leventhal & Tomarken, 1987; Mäkikangas & Kinnunen, 2003; Siegall & Cummings, 1995; Suls & Rittenhouse, 1990; Wiebe & Smith, 1997). As discussed later in this chapter, empirical work has identified a clear role for stress and related mediating processes in explaining the personality-illness relationship.

Chapter 4

THE 'BIG FIVE' TRAITS AND THE PERSONALITY-ILLNESS RELATIONSHIP

Much of the variance in personality can be accounted for by the 'Big Five' factors of extraversion, neuroticism, conscientiousness, agreeableness and openness (Costa & McCrae, 1992; Goldberg, 1993; McCrae & John, 1992). Stone and Costa (1990) described the Five Factor Model (FFM) as a powerful framework for understanding the role of personality in illness and disease. Preliminary support for the Big Five – then labelled Surgency (extraversion), Emotional Stability (neuroticism), Conscientiousness, Agreeableness, and Culture (openness) – first appeared in the early 1960s (Goldberg, 1993; Winter, 1996). However, sporadic support for the Big Five throughout this decade, coupled with a demoralization of personality psychology in the 1970s, meant that the FFM did not emerge as a dominant framework until much later (McCrae & John, 1992). The 1980s saw mounting evidence for the validity of the FFM, and the subsequent development and broad application of the NEO Personality Inventory (NEO-PI) (Costa & McCrae, 1985), and later the NEO-PI Revised and the NEO-FFI (Costa & McCrae, 1992), as major assessment tools for the Big Five (Digman, 1990; McCrae & Costa, 1987; McCrae, Costa & Busch, 1986; Rust, 1999). The NEO-PI-R measures 30 facets or sub-traits classified according to the Big Five domains: (1) Extraversion (activity, assertiveness, excitement seeking, gregariousness, positive emotions, warmth); (2) Neuroticism (angry hostility, anxiety, depression, impulsiveness, self-consciousness, vulnerability); (3) Conscientiousness (achievement striving, competence, deliberation, dutifulness, order, self-discipline); (4) Agreeableness (altruism, compliance, modesty, straightforwardness, tender-mindedness, trust); and (5) Openness (actions, aesthetics, fantasy, feelings, ideas, values).

The role of traits - defined and measured according to the FFM - in the personality-illness relationship is a relatively young research pursuit. Historically, the personality dimension that has received the most attention in this context is 'Type A' behavior pattern (TABP) (Jex, 1998). TABP first came to prominence in the field of cardiology in the 1950s (see Friedman & Rosenman, 1959), based on the observation that people with coronary heart disease (CHD) frequently exhibited 'hurry sickness' e.g., ambitiousness, competitiveness, explosive speech, impatience, irritability, rapid jerky body movement, tense facial and body musculature, time urgency (Dembroski & Costa, 1987; Järvikoski & Härkäpää, 1987; Powell, 1987). TABP was measured on a single dimension from 'Type A' to 'Type B', where Bs exhibited such behavior to a lesser extent. The general argument was that ambitious, hard-driving, Type As were more likely to succeed than their Type B counterparts, but simultaneously risked paying a hefty price in relation to their health (Spence, Helmreich, Pred, 1987).

However, inconsistent evidence for a TABP-CHD relationship led to a re-conceptualization of TABP as a multi-dimensional construct, as opposed to a global coronary-prone behavior pattern (Dembroski, 1985; Ganster, Schaubroeck, Sime & Mayes, 1991; Spence et al., 1987). A distinction was drawn between 'toxic' versus 'protective' Type A behaviors, and attention quickly shifted to hostility as the likely toxic component (Costa, Stone, McCrae, & Dembroski, 1987; Dembroski, 1985; Dembroski & Costa, 1987; MacDougall, Dembroski, Dimsdale, & Hackett, 1985).

There is now considerable evidence to support the view that the relationship between TABP and CHD is dimension-specific (Costa et al., 1987; Dembroski, 1985; Dembroski & Costa, 1987, 1988; Ganster et al., 1991; MacDougall et al., 1985). Spence et al. (1987) identified a two-factor model of Type A behavior, 'achievement striving' and 'impatience-irritability', which subsequently gained popularity in the literature (see e.g., Bluen, Barlin, & Burns, 1990; Lee, 1992; Lee, Ashford, & Jamieson, 1993; Spector & O'Connell, 1994; Spence et al., 1987; Spence, Pred, & Helmreich, 1989; Ward & Eisler, 1987a, 1987b). Achievement striving is positively related to academic and job performance, problem-focused coping, and job satisfaction, suggesting a protective function (see Bluen et al., 1990; Lee, 1992; Lee et al., 1993; Spence et al., 1987; Spence et al., 1989). However, this dimension may be associated with disordered achievement-related self-regulation (Ward & Eisler, 1987a, 1987b). In contrast to achievement striving, impatience-irritability is negatively related to problem-focused coping and job satisfaction, and positively related to depression (see Bluen et al., 1990; Lee, 1992; Lee et al., 1993; Spence et al., 1987; Spence et al., 1989). Within the FFM, achievement striving is captured by the dimension of conscientiousness. Impatience-irritability on the other hand, is captured by neuroticism and antagonism or low agreeableness.

This chapter reviews the literature on the Big Five and the personality-illness relationship, focussing on neuroticism as *the* personality risk factor for stress and impaired health and well-being. Consistent with Suls and Martin (2005), the chapter focuses on neuroticism scores that fall at the high end of the normal personality continuum.

Chapter 5

NEUROTICISM AS A RISK FACTOR FOR STRESS AND IMPAIRED HEALTH AND WELL-BEING

This section focuses on studies of the relationship between personality and physical and mental health outcomes. Explanatory mechanisms underlying the personality-illness relationship are considered later in the chapter.

NEUROTICISM AND PHYSICAL HEALTH

While neuroticism is negatively related to physical health, extraversion, conscientiousness, openness, and agreeableness are generally positively related to physical health. When discussing the relationship between personality and physical health, it is important to distinguish between two different types of studies that exist within this literature: those based on self-reported health outcomes, such as symptom and illness reports or perceived health status, and those based on objective health outcomes, such as diagnosed disorders and diseases or mortality (c.f Smith, 2006). The importance of this distinction is elaborated below.

SELF-REPORTED HEALTH OUTCOMES

Neuroticism has been consistently linked with *self-reported* symptoms and illness. For example, Jerram and Coleman (1999) found that neuroticism was associated with higher self-reported illness, poorer perceived health, and higher physician utilization among the elderly. In contrast, agreeableness and openness were associated with good perceived health, and conscientiousness was associated with higher physician utilization but good perceived health among men, while agreeableness was associated with lower physician utilization and lower self-reported illness among women. Goodwin and Engstrom (2002) found that low neuroticism and high extraversion, conscientiousness, and openness were associated with good perceived health among both healthy and unhealthy respondents.

While self-report measures are convenient, such measures are more likely to indicate illness behavior - behavior associated with the *perception* of illness e.g., absenteeism, physician utilisation, over or under reporting symptoms, self-medicating - as opposed to objective health status per se (Smith & McKenzie, 2006; Wiebe & Smith, 1997).

The association between neuroticism and self-reported symptom and illness reporting may reflect the trait anxiety or negative affectivity (NA) facet of the trait. NA is characterized by a generalized sense of negative emotionality or subjective distress (Watson & Clark, 1984; Watson, Clark, & Tellegen, 1988; Watson & Pennebaker, 1989). Those who score high on NA tend to be introspective, and to dwell on the negative side of themselves, others, and the world in general (Watson & Clark, 1984; Watson & Pennebaker, 1989). As a result, they have a negative self-concept and feel dissatisfied on the whole (Watson & Pennebaker, 1989). As such, NA may increase self-focused attention or somatic concern, leading to a preoccupation with sensation and illness and an increased tendency to perceive, report, or act on sensation as illness (Wiebe & Smith, 1997). Watson and Pennebaker (1989) described NA as a general trait of somatopsychic distress that is associated with a broad range of *self-reported* symptoms. They found that NA was unrelated to objective health status. Recent research has shown that neuroticism is associated with negative aging self-stereotypes, which in turn affect perceived health status (Moor, Zimprich, Schmitt, & Kliegel, 2006).

The relationship between neuroticism and excessive or unfounded symptom and illness reporting is consistent with an *Illness Behavior Model.* According to this model, neuroticism is related to subjective health status via hyper-vigilance and hypochondriasis. However, other studies have refuted a general attentional or recall bias hypothesis. For example, Johnson (2003) found that neuroticism was positively related to tension symptom reporting (e.g., high blood pressure, neck pain, migraine) but was unrelated to asthma or common cold symptom reporting. Stone and Costa (1990) suggested that the disposition to report symptoms in the absence of organic disease may indicate (a) a tendency to worry about health more than usual due to anxiety, depression, or a general vulnerability factor; (b) hyper-sensitivity to pain; (c) a history of reinforcement for adopting a sick role; (d) an illness or disease-prone experience of life and subsequent tendency to perceive, recall and report symptoms in a manner consistent with this; or (e) symptoms that are due to something other than organic disease. According to this view then, the tendency to over-report symptoms can be attributed to individual differences in subjective experience rather than a report bias (Goodwin, Cox, & Clara, 2006).

Objective Health Outcomes

In light of the ambiguities associated with self-reported health outcomes, researchers are increasingly turning their attention to prospective studies of objective health outcomes. Such studies have confirmed that neuroticism does indeed play a genuine role in objective health status.

Several studies have examined the relationship between personality traits and mortality or outcomes associated with the prevalence and course of specific physical disorders or diseases. Wilson et al. (2005) found that high neuroticism (90th percentile) was associated with a 33% increase in risk of death among those aged 65 or older, compared with low neuroticism (10th percentile). High extraversion was also associated with higher risk, although the risk (21%) was substantially lower than for high neuroticism. Adjustment for baseline cognitive, social, and physical activity attenuated the effect of both traits, suggesting that these variables were possible mediators. A recent study of risk of mortality from particular causes (Shipley, Weiss, Der, Taylor, & Deary, 2008) revealed that a one standard deviation increase in neuroticism was associated with a 12% increased risk of death from cardiovascular disease. This remained significant after adjustment for age, gender, occupational social class, education, smoking, alcohol consumption, physical activity, and health. However, neuroticism was not associated with death from lung cancer and other forms of cancer, respiratory disease, or stroke. Extraversion was a protective factor for risk of death from respiratory disease in this study.

Goodwin and Friedman (2006) examined the relationship between the Big Five and common mental and physical disorders among adults in the general population. They found that neuroticism was associated with increased likelihood of a wide range of mental and physical disorders, while conscientiousness was associated with reduced likelihood. A study of the relationship between neuroticism and physical disorders among adults in the general community (Goodwin et al., 2006), showed that neuroticism was associated with increased odds of arthritis (odds ratio [OR] = 1.5), diabetes (OR = 3.33), kidney/liver disease (OR = 2.56), stomach/gallbladder problems (OR = 2.27) and ulcer (OR = 3.23). These associations persisted after adjusting for differences in demographic characteristics and comorbid mental health disorders. A twin study (Charles, Gatz, Kato, & Pedersen, 2008), indicated that the likelihood of having a physical condition at 25-year follow up was related to higher prior neuroticism, although some associations were attenuated when familial similarity was controlled.

Other studies have focused on progression or recovery in relation to specific conditions. A recent study (Ironson, O'Cleirigh, Weiss, Schneiderman, & Costa, 2008) reported that facets within the domains of extraversion (assertiveness, positive emotionality, gregariousness), conscientiousness (achievement striving, order) and openness (ideas, aesthetics) were associated with slower HIV disease progression. In addition, profile analyses indicated that the following 'types' were associated with slower disease progression: low neuroticism plus high extraversion, low neuroticism plus high conscientiousness, high extraversion plus high conscientiousness, high extraversion plus high agreeableness, and high extraversion plus high openness. In contrast, low extraversion plus low openness was associated with faster disease progression. Once again, the results suggest that high neuroticism is a risk factor, while high scores on the remaining traits confer an adaptive effect.

Chung, Berger, Jones, and Rudd (2006) investigated the relationship between personality traits and post-traumatic stress disorder (PTSD) symptoms and health problems in older patients following myocardial infarction (MI). They found that neuroticism predicted all post MI PTSD symptoms as well as general health problems, while low agreeableness (antagonism) predicted hyper-arousal symptoms only. In addition, extraversion, conscientiousness, and openness were unrelated to post-MI PTSD or general health problems. The results remained significant when controlling for angina, angioplasty, bypass surgery, heart failure, and previous mental health problems. The authors noted the consistency between their findings and the general PTSD literature, where neuroticism is the primary personality risk factor for developing PTSD.

Chapter 6

NEUROTICISM AND MENTAL HEALTH

PSYCHOPATHOLOGY

Neuroticism is associated with a range of mental disorders, most notably anxiety, mood, substance, and personality disorders (see e.g., Clark, Watson, & Mineka, 1994; Costa & McCrae, 1990; de Graaf, Bijl, Ravelli, Smit, & Vollenbergh, 2002; Frokjaer et al., 2008; Hirschfeld, Klerman, Lavori, & Keller, 1989; King, Bernardy, & Hauner, 2003; Mangold & Wand, 2006; Weinstock & Whisman, 2006; Zonderman, Herbst, Schmidt, Costa, & McCrae, 1993). In addition, the trait has been linked with first instance of mental disorders in the general population, as well as symptom severity, treatment efficacy, and remission and recovery among psychiatric patients (Goodwin et al., 2006). A full review of the role of personality in mental health is beyond the scope of this chapter. Therefore, the discussion below will focus on personality disorders (PDs) only.

The relationship between broad dimensions of normal personality, as measured by the Five Factor Model, and PDs has become a major focus for research, with an abundance of studies in the past decade (for reviews see Samuel & Widiger, 2008; Saulsman & Page, 2004). Led by Widiger and colleagues, recently there has been considerable discussion of the implications of this research for Diagnostic and Statistical Manual of Mental Disorders, Fifth Edition (DSM-V) (see e.g., Widiger & Samuel, 2005; Widiger, Simonsen, Krueger, Livesley, & Verheul, 2006; Widiger & Lowe, 2008; Widiger & Trull, 2007). For example, are personality disorders best diagnosed using categorical or dimensional models of classification? The basic argument is that PDs can be conceptualized as 'extreme variants' of normal personality dimensions. Widiger and Lowe (2007) highlighted three advantages of a Five-Factor Model of PDs: (a) precise yet comprehensive description of both abnormal and normal personality functioning; (b) avoidance of the limitations/problems inherent in the categorical diagnostic system (e.g., heterogeneous category membership, boundary with normality is unstable, diagnostic co-occurrence); and (c) integration of research on general personality functioning into current description and understanding of PDs.

Saulsman and Page (2004) conducted a meta-analysis of studies examining the relationship between the Big Five domains and the 10 PD diagnostic categories included in DSM-IV: Antisocial, Avoidant, Borderline, Dependent, Histrionic, Narcissistic, Obsessive-Compulsive, Paranoid, Schizoid, and Schizotypal. They examined maladaptive personality domains both within and across PD categories. Findings revealed that (high) neuroticism and (low) agreeableness were common across most PDs (except Dependent), while high or low extraversion and, to a lesser extent high or low conscientiousness, were common to some PDs but not others. In general, effect sizes for neuroticism and agreeableness were substantial and directionally-consistent across the PDs. Neuroticism was positively associated with PDs characterized by emotional distress (Avoidant, Borderline, Dependent, Paranoid, and Schizotypal) and agreeableness was negatively associated with PDs characterized by interpersonal problems (Antisocial, Borderline, Narcisstic, Paranoid, and Schizotypal). For extraversion, PDs characterized by gregariousness showed a positive association (Histrionic and Narcissitic), while those characterized by shyness and withdrawal showed a negative association (Avoidant, Schizoid, Schizotypal). For conscientiousness, PDs associated with orderliness showed a positive association (Obsessive-Compulsive), while those associated with recklessness showed a negative association (Antisocial and Borderline). The magnitude of the effect sizes for each PD indicated that, overall, the Five-Factor Model was better at conceptualizing some PDs (Avoidant and Borderline) than others (Obsessive-Compulsive and Schizoid). Results were generally consistent across both clinical and non-clinical samples. The authors concluded that high neuroticism-low agreeableness is likely to be an issue for a substantial number of PD patients. It may be that low agreeableness exacerbates the effect of high neuroticism on mental ill health.

A limitation of the Saulsman and Page meta-analysis was that it focused on a domain-level analysis, rather than a facet-level analysis based on the 30 sub-traits of the FFM. The authors acknowledged that for some PDs, lower order facets may show a consistent pattern (all high or all low), whereas for other PDs lower order facets may be inconsistent (some high and some low). Notably however there were few facet-level studies available for analysis at the time of this meta-analysis.

Samuel and Widiger (2008) replicated and extended the Saulsman and Page meta-analysis by conducting both a domain-level analysis and a facet-level analysis, using 18 new, independent samples. While the Saulsman and Page meta-analysis indicated that five of the 10 PDs were meaningfully related to neuroticism, Samuel and Widiger found that only one of these PDs (Borderline) correlated above .20 with the impulsivity facet. Furthermore, the Antisocial and Dependent PDs correlated with neuroticism for different reasons: Antisocial PD correlated only with the angry hostility and impulsiveness facets, whereas Dependent PD correlated with the other four facets. Similarly, the Antisocial, Borderline, Paranoid, Narcissistic, and Schizotypal PDs all correlated with low agreeableness, but the facet-level analysis indicated that only one of the PDs (Narcissistic) was associated with the modesty facet. The authors concluded that PDs may be associated with the same FFM domain but for largely different reasons. On the basis of their findings, they suggested that the five global domains may be too broad to have diagnostic utility.

The development of explanatory models of the relationship between personality traits and psychopathology is in its infancy. The question remains as to how neuroticism, agreeableness and extraversion are maladaptive among those with PDs. Saulsman and Page (2004) noted that extreme scores on personality traits are not sufficient for the development of PDs. Clark (2005) proposed that innate temperament dimensions interact with life stress to differentiate into risk factors for psychopathology through developmental pathways.

WELL-BEING

A discussion of the relationship between personality and mental health would not be complete without considering dimensions of psychological functioning in the general population. Well-being is an important index of psychological functioning and quality of life, and represents a desired mental state for most people (Schmutte & Ryff, 1997; Siegrist, 2003). Based on the current conceptulization in the literature, well-being can be defined as a multi-dimensional construct consisting of both hedonic and eudaimonic dimensions (Ryan & Deci, 2001). Hedonic or 'subjective well-being' includes the dimensions of negative affect, positive affect, and life satisfaction (Diener, 1984; Diener, Oishi, & Lucas, 2003; Lucas, Diener, & Suh, 1996). Domain-specific measures of satisfaction, such as job satisfaction, may also be used (see Grant & Langan-Fox, 2007). In contrast, eudiamonic or 'psychological well-being' is based on a broader approach which includes autonomy, environmental mastery, personal growth, positive relations, purpose in life, and self-acceptance (see Deci & Ryan, 2006; Ryff, 1989; Ryff & Singer, 1996).

The relationship between personality and subjective well-being has been widely studied, with two major meta-analyses in the past 10 years. A meta-analysis (DeNeve & Cooper, 1998) of the relationship between 137 distinct personality constructs and subjective well-being found that when personality traits were grouped according to the Big Five, neuroticism was the strongest predictor of negative affect (.23) and life satisfaction (-.24), however extraversion and agreeableness were the strongest predictors of positive affect (.20 and .17 respectively). More recently, Steel, Schmidt, and Shultz (2008) performed a separate meta-analysis of the relationship between personality and subjective well-being, based only on the NEO-PI. They reported substantially larger meta-analytic correlations than those reported by DeNeve and Cooper, suggesting that combining disparate measures of the Big Five within the same analysis may attenuate the relationship between the traits and subjective well-being. Consistent with DeNeve and Cooper, neuroticism was the strongest correlate of negative affect (.54) and life satisfaction (-.38), and extraversion was the strongest correlate of positive affect (.44).

VittersØ (2001) argued that it is important to identify the unique contribution of neuroticism and extraversion to subjective well-being, given that the two traits are typically correlated, particularly within the FFM. VittersØ found that when neuroticism was controlled in multiple regression analysis, the effect of extraversion on subjective well-being was substantially diminished or disappeared altogether. In a similar study, Hills and Argyle (2001) investigated the relationship of emotional stability (the positive analogue to neuroticism) and extraversion to happiness. They found that happiness was more strongly related to emotional stability than to extraversion, with emotional stability accounting for a greater proportion of the total variability explained in multiple regression analysis.

Consistent with the subjective well-being literature, neuroticism and extraversion have also emerged as major correlates of psychological well-being. However, the other three traits, and in particular conscientiousness, are also important in this context. A study (Siegler & Brumment, 2000) of facet-psychological well-being correlations indicated that over 80% of the correlations within the domains of neuroticism, extraversion and conscientiousness were significant, compared with less than half of the correlations within the domains of agreeableness and openness.

Adjusting for various spurious effects (i.e., common affective underpinnings, shared item content and source overlap), Schmutte and Ryff (1997) found that neuroticism was negatively related to autonomy, environmental mastery, purpose in life and self-acceptance; extraversion was positively related to all dimensions of psychological well-being except autonomy; conscientiousness was positively related to environmental mastery, purpose in life, and self-acceptance; and agreeableness and openness were positively related to positive relations and personal growth respectively.

A factor analysis of the Big Five and well-being dimensions (van Dierendonck, 2005) revealed four factors: a well-being factor on which all subjective and psychological well-being scales loaded with neuroticism; a self-actualization factor consisting of personal growth, purpose in life and conscientiousness; an interpersonal relations factor consisting of positive relations and extraversion and agreeableness, and a fourth factor consisting of autonomy and openness.

A study (Bardi & Ryff, 2007) of the combined/interactive effect of neuroticism and other traits in the prediction of psychological well-being following relocation, found that participants who scored low on neuroticism and high on openness reported higher environmental mastery and self-acceptance one month after relocation, and higher personal growth late in the post-relocation adjustment process. In addition, neuroticism had a significant main effect on all six aspects of psychological well-being, predicting lower post-move well-being scores.

Together, these studies suggest that neuroticism is consistently related to all dimensions, except personal growth; extraversion is consistently related to environmental mastery, positive relations, purpose in life, and self-acceptance; conscientiousness is consistently related to environmental mastery, purpose in life and self-acceptance; and agreeableness is consistently related to positive relations.

Other studies have examined the relationship between the Big Five and subjective and psychological well-being simultaneously. Keyes, Shmotkin, and Ryff (2002) found that people who scored low on both subjective and psychological well-being had the highest average for neuroticism and the lowest average for extraversion and conscientiousness. In contrast, those who scored high on both subjective and psychological well-being demonstrated the opposite trait profile. Openness distinguished between types with high psychological well-being but low subjective well-being, and types with low psychological well-being but high subjective well-being.

Grant, Langan-Fox and Anglim (under review) examined the relationship between personality and well-being using a structured model comparison approach. Nested models were compared with the aim of answering the following research questions: (1) Does the size of the relationship between personality and well-being differ for subjective versus psychological well-being? (2) Does the size of the relationship between personality and well-being differ for particular personality traits? (3) Does the relationship between particular personality traits and well-being differ for subjective versus psychological well-being? (4) Given a particular personality trait (e.g., neuroticism), is the relationship between that trait larger for some well-being dimensions (e.g., negative affect) than for others? That is, is the relationship larger than the average personality-well-being relationship for that trait? They found that, overall, the relationship between personality and well-being was larger for psychological well-being than for subjective well-being. However, neuroticism showed a similar relationship to subjective and psychological well-being, and extraversion and conscientiousness showed a slightly stronger relationship with psychological well-being. Agreeableness showed a stronger relationship with subjective well-being than with psychological well-being, while openness showed a stronger relationship with psychological well-being. An examination of the overall relationship between the personality traits and well-being revealed that neuroticism showed the largest relationship with well-being, followed by extraversion, conscientiousness, openness and agreeableness in that order. Furthermore, neuroticism was the strongest correlate of both subjective and psychological well-being. Positive affect and negative affect showed larger than average correlations with extraversion and neuroticism respectively; personal growth showed a larger than average correlation with openness; positive relations showed larger than average correlations with extraversion and agreeableness; and purpose in life showed larger than average correlations with conscientiousness. Environmental mastery and self-acceptance were not examined in this study.

Chapter 7

EXPLANATORY MECHANISMS: MEDIATING PROCESSES IN THE PERSONALITY-ILLNESS RELATIONSHIP

Research on stress has made an important contribution to our current understanding of the role of personality in health and well-being,

> "The association of increased stress with various illnesses is the single most important finding in convincing adherents to the medico-mechanical model of disease that psychosocial factors may play a role in the etiology of illness" (McClelland, 1985, p. 455).

The remainder of this chapter focuses on an overarching process model, describing the effect of neuroticism on various intermediate mechanisms that tie situational stressors to health and well-being. This model can be summarized as follows:

NEUROTICISM
↓

Stressor exposure → Cognitive appraisal → (Stress →) Coping → Reactivity → Health / Well-being
Health behavior

The various subsections below outline how neuroticism is implicated in each of these phases of the stressor-illness process. Note that research on stressor exposure and reactivity is reviewed in the same section, given that studies have typically examined these two variables concurrently.

NEUROTICISM AND STRESSOR EXPOSURE AND REACTIVITY

Several studies indicate that neurotics report greater exposure to stressful life events and daily hassles (David, Green, Martin, & Suls, 1997; Fergusson and Horwood, 1987; Gunthert, Cohen, & Armelli, 1999; Magnus, Diener, Fujita, & Payot, 1993; Ormel & Wohlfarth, 1991; Poulton and Andrews, 1992; Zautra, Afflect, Tennen, Reich, & Davis, 2005) and are more likely to react to these stressors with emotional distress (Brow, 2008; Bolger & Shilling, 1991; Bolger & Zuckerman, 1995; Malyszczak et al., 2007; Marco & Suls, 1993; Suls, Martin, & David, 1998; Zautra et al., 2005). For example, longitudinal research has shown that neuroticism is associated with greater exposure to stressful life events during adulthood (Fergusson & Horwood, 1987; Magnus et al., 1993), and a daily diary study (Bolger & Schilling, 1991) found that neuroticism was associated with greater exposure to stressors, greater emotional reactivity to these stressors, and greater distress in general. Malyszczak et al. (2007) reported that patients with higher neuroticism scores were more likely to develop psychological distress under stress caused by somatic illness. A recent study (Brow, 2008) of stress in the wake of 9/11 revealed that neuroticism was associated with greater emotional distress.

Neuroticism is also associated with stressor exposure within particular life domains, such as the work and interpersonal domains. For example, neuroticism has been linked with higher occupational stress among managers (Ahmad, James, & Ahmad, 1991) and medical consultants (Deary et al., 1996), and higher acculturative stress among international students (Duru & Poyrazli, 2007; Mangold, Veraza, Kinker, & Kinney, 2007). One study (Andreassi, 2007) found that neuroticism predicted higher scores on four measures of work-family conflict (work-to-family, family-to-work, strain-based, and time-based), while extraversion was unrelated to the four outcome measures. Neuroticism has also been linked with higher exposure to interpersonal conflict (Bolger & Zuckerman, 1995) and other negative relationship outcomes (Karney & Bradbury, 1995; Hellmuth, & McNulty, 2008). Zautra et al. (2005) found that neuroticism was associated with negative events, relationship stress, and negative affect but was unrelated to positive events or relationship enjoyment. In contrast, extraversion was associated with positive events, relationship enjoyment, and positive affect, but was unrelated to negative events, relationship stress, and negative affect. In addition, neuroticism exacerbated the effect of a day's negative events on negative affectivity.

A study of the relationship between the Big Five and emotional reactivity to daily hassles (Suls, Green, & Hillis, 1998) found that those who scored high on neuroticism reported greater exposure and emotional reactivity to daily hassles, and greater distress in relation to recurrent hassles than those who scored lower on neuroticism. In addition, high neuroticism and low agreeableness were associated with a lagged-effect of prior (negative) mood on distress. In contrast, extraversion, conscientiousness and openness were unrelated to emotional reactivity or distress.

Studies of personality and physiological reactivity to stress typically focus on cardiovascular reactivity or immune system functioning (Friedman, 2000). Chida and Hamer (2008) found that neuroticism was associated with decreased cardiovascular reactivity but poor cardiovascular recovery in response to stress. Findings were explained in terms of a heightened orienting response, whereby neurotics are highly attentive to external stimuli and therefore exhibit a reduction in stressor reactivity but persistence of physiological arousal after the stressor has been removed. Other studies have shown that neuroticism is associated with blunted cortisol reactivity in response to acute stress and poor antibody response (Phillips, Carroll, Burns, & Drayson, 2005).

In recent years, several studies have utilized Vollrath and Torgersen's (2000) 8 personality types to examine the combined effect of neuroticism, extraversion and conscientiousness on stressor exposure (Grant & Langan-Fox, 2006; Lau, Hem, Berg, Ekeberg, & Torgersen, 2006; Tyssen et al., 2007). The 8 types represent unique configurations of high and low neuroticism, extraversion, and conscientiousness. Although the dichotomization of continuous personality variables into 'high' and 'low' categories can compromise predictive power due to loss of information (Rovik et al., 2007), the general thesis is that examining the interplay of traits (typological approach) provides a more comprehensive and detailed picture of personality than single trait models (dimensional approach), thus enabling the more reliable identification of those at risk (Tyssen et al., 2007). Two studies have shown that types characterized by high neuroticism and low conscientiousness report higher stressor exposure (Vollrath and Torgersen, 2000; Grant & Langan-Fox, 2006). A study of stress during medical school training (Tyssen et al., 2007) found that types combining high neuroticism with low extraversion and high conscientiousness were at risk for experiencing more stress, whereas types combining low neuroticism with high extraversion and low conscientiousness were protected against stress. Similarly, Lau et al. (2006) reported that the combination of low neuroticism and high extraversion was associated with lower stress among police officers, while the combination of high neuroticism and low extraversion was associated with higher stress in this context.

Explaining the Neuroticism-Stressor Exposure and Reactivity Link

Bolger and Zuckerman (1995) proposed that personality traits may influence (i) stressor exposure only (*Differential Exposure Model*), (ii) reactivity only (*Differential Reactivity Model*), or (iii) both exposure and reactivity (*Differential Exposure-Reactivity Model*). According to the Differential Exposure Model, personality influences stressor exposure but once these stressful events occur, everyone reacts in the same way. This model is consistent with a mediated effect model in which personality predicts higher stressor exposure which in turn predicts higher strain or illness. In contrast, the Differential Reactivity Model is based on a moderated effect model in which personality predicts reactivity to stressors and therefore moderates the effect of stressor exposure on strain. The research on neuroticism cited above is consistent with a Differential Exposure-Reactivity Model (Bolger & Zuckerman, 1995), with the trait affecting both the stressor exposure and reactivity phases of the stress-strain process, thereby increasing susceptibility to stress-related illness and disease through both mediated and moderated pathways. It may be that neurotics elicit more frequent, severe, or prolonged stressful events through their own cognitive styles and behavior (c.f. Lemos-Giráldez & Fidalgo-Aliste, 1997; Suls & Rittenhouse, 1990; Wiebe & Smith, 1997). For example, dysfunctional thinking patterns associated with neuroticism may impair decision making, leading to conflict or other problems that increase stressor exposure (Suls & Martin, 2005). It is also possible that neurotics are more likely to self-select (or be selected) into high pressure jobs or dysfunctional interpersonal settings.

An alternative explanation is that neuroticism predicts perceived stress (stress perception hypothesis) rather than external stressor exposure per se (differential exposure hypothesis; Conard & Matthews, 2008). Since stressor exposure is typically assessed via self-report measures, it may be that neurotics do not experience more negative events at all but simply have a lower threshold for appraising events as negative (Suls & Martin, 2005). For example, chronic negative emotionally may mean that neurotics are more likely to notice and recall negative information. Suls and Martin (2005) recommended the use of informants as a potential strategy for tackling this methodological problem.

The effect of neuroticism on reactivity could arise from its influence on (i) coping strategy choice (*Differential Coping Choice Model*), (ii) coping strategy effectiveness (*Differential Coping Effectiveness Model*), or (iii) both coping strategy choice and effectiveness (*Differential Choice-Effectiveness Model*) (Bolger & Zuckerman, 1995). In the Differential Coping Choice Model, the effect of personality on reactivity is mediated by coping choice: Personality predicts differential choice of coping strategies and these strategies in turn lead to different health outcomes. In other words, once particular coping strategies are chosen, these are equally as effective (or ineffective) for everyone. Thus, neurotics may simply choose maladaptive coping strategies in response to stressful events, which in turn lead to poor health outcomes. In the Differential Coping Effectiveness Model, personality moderates the effect of coping on reactivity. According to this model then, neurotics may experience more reactivity following a stressful event not because they routinely choose maladaptive strategies but because they choose strategies that are ineffective for them alone. Alternatively, it may be that neurotics try potentially effective coping strategies but fail to persist with these due to low self-efficacy or chronic negative affect (Suls & Martin, 2005; Tyssen et al., 2007). The relationship between neuroticism and coping is discussed in more detail later in the chapter.

Another possibility is that the effect of neuroticism on reactivity reflects the presence of an underlying third variable, such as an in-born defect or deficit that is responsible for both the overt expression of neurotic traits, and the tendency to react more to stress (Friedman & Booth-Kewley, 1987; Suls & Rittenhouse, 1990; Wiebe & Smith, 1997). According to this *Constitutional Predisposition Model*, neuroticism is a *marker* rather than a maker of vulnerability (Suls & Rittenhouse, 1990). Recent work has supported the link between neuroticism and autonomic nervous system deregulation, and genetics appear to be least partially responsible for this effect (see Riese et al., 2007). A final possibility is that hyper-reactivity increases neuroticism. However, neuroticism is likely to have causal precedence (Suls & Martin, 2005). For example, Suls and Martin suggested that the vulnerability of neurotics is likely to be rooted in biological or learned sensitivity to negative stimuli, for instance heredity or early socialization. They noted that the vulnerability of neurotics seems to extend to all types of stressors while other dimensions of personality, such as low agreeableness, are associated with hyper-reactivity to particular kinds of problems only.

Chapter 8

Neuroticism and Cognitive Appraisal

In addition to showing greater stressor exposure and reactivity, neurotics are also more likely to appraise events as stressful and difficult to manage. A study of primary appraisal among students (Gallagher, 1990) found that neuroticism was positively related to threat appraisal and negatively related to challenge appraisal. In contrast, extraversion showed a positive but weaker relationship with challenge appraisal. Hemenover and Dienstbier (1996) found that students who scored high on neuroticism and low on extraversion rated an exam stressor as more threatening (primary appraisal) and more difficult to cope with (secondary appraisal). Similarly, neuroticism was positively related to appraised threat and stressfulness among prospective students preparing to take a law school entry exam (Maxim, 2000). In the occupational context, Deary et al. (1996) found that (negative) cognitive appraisal and emotion-focused coping mediated the effect of neuroticism on self-reported stress.

Other studies have examined the effect of all Big Five traits on cognitive appraisal simultaneously. A study of caregivers (Watson & Hubbard, 1996) found that neuroticism had a negative effect on secondary appraisal while the remaining traits generally had the opposite effect. Neuroticism was inversely related to perceived control and problem-solving confidence, as well as an overall factor of perceived problem-solving ability. In contrast, conscientiousness was positively related to perceived control, problem-solving confidence, and problem-solving ability. Extraversion and openness showed a positive relationship with perceived problem-solving confidence and problem-solving ability, and agreeableness was positively related to perceived problem-solving ability only. Penley and Tomaka (2002) examined the relationship between the Big Five and cognitive appraisal in relation to an acute stressor: preparing and presenting a speech on a controversial topic. Neuroticism was associated with negative secondary appraisal, whereas conscientiousness and openness were associated with positive primary appraisal, and extraversion, conscientiousness and openness were associated with positive secondary appraisal. In addition, neuroticism was positively correlated with perceived (post task) stress, while extraversion, conscientiousness, and openness were negatively correlated with this outcome variable.

Explaining the Neuroticism - Cognitive Appraisal Link

According to reward sensitivity theory, neuroticism and extraversion capture individual differences in the functioning of two different brain systems: the Behavioral Inhibition System (BIS) and the Behavioral Approach System (BAS) respectively (Smillie, Pickering, & Jackson, 2006). The BIS causes the person to move away from goals in anticipation of an emotional punishment and the BAS causes the person move toward goals in anticipation of an emotional reward (McAdams, 2009). This theory suggests that the relationship between neuroticism and primary appraisal could reflect a selective attention bias or underlying appraisal tendency. That is, those who score high on neuroticism may be ‘punishment sensitive’, selectively attending to potential negative outcomes i.e., threat/damage or loss (Gallagher, 1990; Hemenover and Dienstbier, 1996). In contrast, those who score high on extraversion may be ‘reward sensitive’, selectively attending to potential positive outcomes i.e., challenge. Indeed, Hemenover (2001) found that the neuroticism-cognitive appraisal relationship was mediated by a self-reported tendency to rely on negative information and that the extraversion-cognitive appraisal relationship was mediated by a self-reported tendency to rely on positive information. Kuppens and Van Mechelen (2007) suggested that neurotics are more sensitive to potential personal threats present in unpleasant evaluative events. They found that neuroticism was associated with higher appraised threats to self-esteem.

With regard to neuroticism and secondary appraisal, the negative effect of neuroticism on perceived coping ability may indicate a depletion of coping resources, due to the ongoing management of chronic negative emotionality. Alternatively, it may be that neurotics have fewer coping strategies available to them to begin with (Revenson, 1990). The original formulation of the Transactional Model of Stress and Coping conceptualized coping as a discrete, situation-specific response, however it is now reocgnized that coping is more likely to be 'dispositional' or trait-like in nature (Carver, Scheier, & Weintraub, 1989; Cox & Ferguson, 1991; Dewe et al., 1993; Newton & Keenan, 1990). Indeed, Carver and Scheier (1994) found that dispositional coping was a significant predictor of situational coping.

Dispositional coping is defined as "a characteristic or typical manner of approaching or confronting a stressful situation and dealing with it" (Endler, 1997, p. 143). As discussed in the next section, neuroticism is typically associated with maladaptive and ineffective coping (e.g., Deary et al., 1996; Fickcova, 2001; McCrae & Costa, 1986; Shewchuck, Elliott, MacNair-Semands, & Harkins, 1999). As such, neurotics may feel less efficacious in the face of stressful events, based on past coping experience.

The relationship between neuroticism and cognitive appraisal is consistent with a *Stress Moderation Model* of the personality-illness relationship (Wiebe & Smith, 1997). Within this model, personality is theorized to (i) attenuate, exacerbate, or prevent the appraisal of a situation as stressful, and/or (ii) guide the selection of more or less adaptive coping strategies in response to stressful events, thus influencing physiological reactivity and subsequent health outcomes (Wiebe & Smith, 1997, Suls & Rittenhouse, 1990). Statistically, this model can be represented as a mediated, moderated effect model, in that personality moderates the effect of stressor exposure on strain, an effect mediated by cognitive appraisal.

Chapter 9

NEUROTICISM AND COPING

While there are several typologies of coping strategies, a certain level of convergence has emerged around the broad theoretical distinction between problem-focused and emotion-focused coping strategies (Dewe et al., 1993; Folkman & Lazarus, 1980; Ingledew, Hardy, Cooper, & Jemal, 1996). The former aim to alter or manage stressful events; the latter aim to regulate the emotional distress associated with such events. Emotion-focused coping is often subdivided into (a) reappraisal strategies, which aim to manage interpretation of the stressful event e.g., 'making the best of a bad situation', and (b) avoidance strategies, which aim to minimize tension by evading the stressful event (Bowman & Stern, 1995; Cook & Hepner, 1997; Cox & Ferguson, 1991). Avoidance coping strategies include person-oriented strategies, such as social diversion, and task-oriented strategies, such as distraction (Endler & Parker, 1994). Problem-focused coping may be more adaptive when the stressor is changeable or controllable, while emotion-focused coping may be more adaptive when the stressor must be accepted and endured (Forsythe & Compas, 1987; Lazarus, 1990). Avoidance forms of emotion-focused coping are generally considered to be maladaptive. While avoidance coping may be effective in the short-term, it is likely to lead to poor adjustment in the long-term (Hobfoll, 1988). For example, avoidance coping may be difficult to maintain when stressor exposure is chronic or ongoing, such as in the occupational context (Bowman & Stern, 1995). Indeed, studies have shown that avoidance coping exacerbates the effect of job-related stress on strain (Long, 1993; Parasuraman & Cleek, 1984).

If coping is governed by dispositional styles rather than situation-specific strategies, then it seems reasonable to assume that stable personality traits account for some of the stability in coping (Bouchard, 2003). Indeed, past research has consistently shown that neuroticism is positively related to emotion-focused and avoidance coping and negatively related to problem-focused coping (see e.g., Bouchard, 2003; Deary et al., 1996; Hooker, Frazier, & Monhan, 1994; Matthews et al., 1996; O'Brien & De Longis, 1996; Vollrath, Torgersen, & Alnæs, 1995; Watson & Hubbard, 1996). For example, an early study (McCrae & Costa, 1986) found that neuroticism was positively related to escapist fantasy, hostility, indecisiveness, passivity, sedation, self-blame, wishful thinking, and withdrawal, all of which were perceived as ineffective in relation to problem-solving and distress reduction. In addition, these strategies were negatively related to well-being. Subsequent studies have reported similar findings: O'Brien and DeLongis (1996) found that neurotics reported more escape-avoidance and confrontive coping and less planful problem solving; Fickova (2001) reported an association between neuroticism and maladaptive and ineffective coping among adolescents; and Penley and Tomaka (2002) found that neuroticism was positively related to emotional regulation and defensive coping among students. More recently, Brow (2008) reported that neuroticism was positively related to use of maladaptive coping strategies, such as denial and self-blame, and inversely related to effective coping strategies, such as acceptance and active coping, in the immediate aftermath of 9/11.

Studies using the COPE Inventory (Carver et al., 1989), a widely used measure of coping, have shown that neuroticism is positively correlated with behavioral disengagement, denial, mental disengagement, substance use, and venting, and negatively correlated with active coping, planning, positive reinterpretation, and suppression of competing activities in both clinical and non-clinical samples (Vollrath et al., 1995; Watson & Hubbard, 1996). A recent study of parents rearing children with disabilities (Glidden, Billings, & Jobe, 2006) found that neuroticism was associated with accepting responsibility (self-blame) and escape-avoidance. Escape-avoidance in turn predicted higher depression and lower current and child-related subjective well-being.

Conscientiousness has also emerged as a powerful predictor of coping. In fact, conscientiousness was the strongest Big Five predictor of coping in the Fickova (2001) study. In contrast to neuroticism however, this trait is positively related to problem-focused coping and negatively related to avoidance coping (e.g., Deary et al., 1996; Hooker et al., 1994; Matthews et al., 2006; O'Brien & De Longis, 1996; Penley & Tomaka, 2002; Watson & Hubbard, 1996). For example, Watson and Hubbard (1996) found that conscientiousness was positively related to active coping, planning, and suppression of competing activities, and negatively related to behavioral disengagement, escape-avoidance, mental disengagement, and substance use. The positive relationship between conscientiousness and problem-focused coping has been replicated in the occupational context (see e.g., Deary et al., 1996) and is consistent with the goal-directed and self-disciplined nature of those who score high on this trait (Penley & Tomaka, 2002).

Extraversion is positively related to emotional and instrumental social support seeking (e.g., Amirkan, Risinger, & Swickert, 1995; Fickova, 2001; Hooker et al., 1994; Vollrath et al., 1995; Watson & Hubbard, 1996), however its overall relationship with coping is somewhat inconsistent. For example, when controlling for other traits, O'Brien and De Longis (1996) found that extraversion failed to demonstrate an independent effect on coping, and Penley and Tomaka (2002) found that extraversion was unrelated to coping. In contrast, McCrae and Costa (1986) found that extraversion was positively related to positive thinking, rational action, restraint, and substitution, all of which were perceived as effective in relation to problem-solving and distress reduction.

The relationship between agreeableness and coping is modest. This trait is positively and consistently related to social support seeking, and positively (though less consistently) related to problem-focused and emotion-focused coping (e.g., Hooker et al., 1994; O'Brien & DeLongis, 1996; Penley & Tomaka, 2002). Watson and Hubbard (1996) found that agreeableness was positively related to planning, positive reinterpretation, and negatively related to substance use. In contrast, Fickova (2001) reported a weak relationship between agreeableness and coping. Penley and Tomaka (2002) found that agreeableness was positively related to passive endurance, which they interpreted as consistent with the compliant nature of those who score high on this trait.

Openness is related to a range of coping strategies, though notably some research has reported a weak association. In an early study, McCrae and Costa (1986) found that openness was negatively related to turning to religion, a finding that was later replicated by Watson and Hubbard (1996). In addition, openness was positively related to humour in the McCrae and Costa (1986) study, and positively related to planning and positive reinterpretation, and negatively related to escape-avoidance in the Watson and Hubbard (1996) study. Consistent with Watson and Hubbard (1996), O'Brien and DeLongis (1996) found that openness was positively related to positive reappraisal, while Penley and Tomaka (2002) found that openness was positively correlated with active coping and negatively correlated with passive endurance. A study of coping with marital problems (Bouchard, 2003) found that openness was positively related to planful problem solving.

A recent meta-analysis of the personality and coping literature (Connor-Smith & Flachsbart, 2007) indicated that all Big Five traits predicted specific strategies. Neuroticism predicted less problem-solving and cognitive restructuring, whereas extraversion and conscientiousness showed the opposite pattern. In addition, neuroticism predicted dysfunctional coping strategies such as wishful thinking, withdrawal, and maladaptive forms of emotion-focused coping but, along with extraversion, it also predicted support seeking. In addition, personality was a stronger predictor of coping in younger samples, stressed samples, and samples that reported dispositional rather than situational coping.

Given that neuroticism, extraversion, and conscientiousness tend to show the strongest association with coping, some studies have examined the combined effect of these three traits. Such studies suggest that personality types that combine high neuroticism with low conscientiousness report less problem-focused coping and more avoidance coping than other types (Grant & Langan-Fox, 2006; Vollrath & Torgersen, 2000).

Explaining the Neuroticism-Coping Link

The relationship between neuroticism and coping is consistent with the Differential Coping Choice and Stress Moderation models described earlier. That is, neurotics appear to choose passive and maladaptive coping strategies, such as venting and avoidance coping, in response to stress. Thus, neuroticism moderates the effect of stressor exposure on strain, an effect mediated by coping.

The choice of emotion-focused coping strategies among neurotics may be driven by chronic emotionality, with neurotics preferring to use strategies that regulate emotional distress (Terry, 1994 cited in Bouchard, 2003). Connor-Smith and Flachsbart (2007) suggested that personality may influence coping strategy choice via stressor exposure. For example, given that neurotics report higher stressor exposure, they may choose avoidance coping strategies to escape from an abundance of stressors, whereas those who experience lower stressor exposure may be better placed to use other strategies. The strong and consistent relationship between neuroticism and avoidance coping could also be driven by the anxiety facet of the trait (Tyssen et al., 2007).

Chapter 10

NEUROTICISM AND HEALTH BEHAVIOR

Health behavior refers to any behavior that has a consequence for health, though not necessarily as a goal e.g., adherence to prescribed medical treatment, diet/eating, drinking, exercise, general self-care, preventative health care e.g., medical screening, relaxation, sexual promiscuity, sleeping, substance use, thrill seeking etc. (Friedman, 2000; Ingledew et al., 1996). There is some evidence that personality precipitates dangerous or risky health behavior (Lemos-Giráldez & Fidalgo-Aliste, 1997; Suls & Rittenhouse, 1990), with neuroticism once again exerting a negative or maladaptive effect. Vingerhoets, Croon, Jeninga, and Menges (1990) found that adults who scored higher on neuroticism demonstrated poorer everyday health behavior (i.e., sleeping, breakfast, snacking, good weight, smoking, alcohol, physical activity) than those who scored lower on neuroticism. Similarly, Booth-Kewley and Vickers (1994) found that neuroticism was negatively related to wellness behavior (e.g., exercise, healthy diet, vitamin intake) and accident control, and positively related to risk taking. Conversely, conscientiousness and agreeableness were positively related to wellness behavior and accident control, and negatively related to risk taking. Openness was also associated with greater substance-related risk taking, and was the only significant predictor of this aspect of health behavior, suggesting that it also has a maladaptive effect in this context. Peltzer (2004) found that neuroticism and psychoticism were inversely related to preventative health behavior, while optimism was positively related to health behavior.

There is some evidence to suggest that the link between personality and health behavior is established early, with some gender-specific differences. A study of the relationship between personality and risky behavior in children

(Markey, Markey, Ericksen, & Tinsley, 2006) indicated that risky behavior among girls was related to behavior patterns associated with neuroticism, introversion and disagreeableness, while risky behavior among boys was related to behavior patterns associated with extraversion and disagreeableness. A longitudinal study of adulthood predictors of health-promoting behavior in aging (Holahan & Suzuki, 2004) found that neuroticism was negatively related to positive psychosocial behavior, while easygoingness was positively related to positive psychosocial behavior and health practices. There is also some evidence to suggest that health behaviors mediate between neuroticism and depressive symptoms (see Gallant & Connell, 2003).

While the bulk of evidence suggests that neuroticism is associated with risky health behavior, one study (Vollrath, Knoch, & Cassano, 1999) has reported conflicting findings. Vollrath et al. (1999) investigated the relationship between personality and (a) perceived susceptibility to health risks and (b) risky health behavior (being drunk, drunk driving, risky sexual behavior, smoking) among university students. Neuroticism was positively correlated with perceived susceptibility to three of the four health risks; however path models indicated that this higher perceived susceptibility could not be explained by a higher frequency of risky health behavior. In fact, those who scored high on neuroticism engaged in less risky health behavior. In other words, they tended to worry about health risks despite being no better or worse in terms of their actual health behavior. Agreeableness was the most consistent predictor of perceived susceptibility to health risks and risky health behavior, such that those who scored high on this trait were more optimistic about future health risks and engaged in less risky health behavior. Findings for conscientiousness were similar to those for agreeableness. Openness was unrelated to perceived susceptibility to health risks and actual risky health behavior.

Friedman's (2000) commentary on the mechanisms underlying the relationship between neuroticism and health behavior helps to reconcile these inconsistent findings. Friedman suggested that neuroticism can lead people down two alternate pathways: On the one hand, pessimism, resentment, and anxiety may lead neurotics to give up on medical regimens, turn to substance abuse, and avoid interpersonal assistance. On the other hand, vigilance about symptoms, advancement in medical practices, and adherence to treatment may lead neurotics to avoid risky health behavior. These differential outcomes are likely to be influenced by stress: Based on an analysis of data from the Terman Life Cycle Study, Friedman found that neurotics who faced parental divorce as children were at increased risk for premature mortality.

With regard to the combined effect of neuroticism, extraversion and conscientiousness on health behavior, types combining high neuroticism with high extraversion or low conscientiousness engage in more alcohol and drug abuse, drunk-driving, smoking, and risky sexual behavior (Vollrath & Torgersen, 2002, 2008). High extraversion-low conscientiousness types also demonstrate more risky behavior.

Other typological studies have focused on the combination of high neuroticism with low extraversion, or the so-called 'Type D' personality. Denollet (1997) identified Type Ds as a coronary heart disease (CHD) subgroup characterized by problems with negative emotionality and self-expression and depressive symptoms. Williams, O'Brien, and Colder (2004) found that the combination of high neuroticism and low extraversion predicted poorer health behavior *self-efficacy*. Controlling for the main effect of neuroticism, Type Ds reported significantly less health behavior and less social support than non-Type Ds. Williams et al. concluded that health behavior may play a role in explaining the link between Type D and poor clinical prognosis among cardiac patients.

EXPLAINING THE NEUROTICISM-HEALTH BEHAVIOR LINK

The relationship between personality and health behavior may reflect individual differences in how people respond to social regulation (Tucker, Elliot, & Klein, 2006). For example, neurotics may react more negatively to overt attempts by others to influence their health behavior (Tucker et al., 2006). In contrast, conscientiousness people may willingly practice positive health behavior, due to a sense of obligation and responsibility to others. Indeed, people who score high on conscientiousness tend to internalize societal norms regarding sensible health-related behavior and to adhere to prescribed treatment recommendations (Goodman & Friedman, 2006).

An alternative explanation is that neurotics engage in risky health behavior as a means of dealing with stress. Coping strategies may include positive health behavior, such as exercise, or negative health behavior, such substance use (Gallant & Connell, 2003), which is typically conceptualized as a form of avoidance coping (Ingledew et al., 1996). In the *Health Behavior Model*, a specialized version of the Stress Moderation Model discussed above, personality is thought to guide the selection of more or less adaptive *health-*

related coping strategies in response to stress, thus influencing physiological arousal and subsequent health outcomes (Wiebe & Smith, 1997). In addition, some health behavior may be directly beneficial or detrimental to health, over and above any stress moderating effect (Ingledew et al., 1996). For example, regular planned exercise to reduce tension may have a direct, positive effect on health (Ingledew et al., 1996). Conversely, while alcohol and drug use may temporarily numb psychological distress, excessive and routine use, such as in conjunction with chronic stress, may have a direct, negative effect on health (Begley, 1998; Lepore, 1995). In support of the Health Behavior Model, Korotkov (2008) found that emotional stability, introversion, conscientiousness and openness were associated with higher engagement in health practices under high stress/distress.

CONCLUSION

In summary, neuroticism is associated with a range of physical conditions as well as psychopathology and impaired well-being. In addition, neuroticism has been linked with heightened stressor exposure, negative cognitive appraisal, maladaptive coping, risky health behavior, and exaggerated emotional reactivity. These findings suggest that neuroticism may influence health and well-being indirectly, via stressor exposure or risky health behavior, or in interaction with stressful events by moderating their effect on health and well-being, via cognitive appraisal, coping, or reactivity (Bolger & Shilling, 1991; Bolger & Zuckerman, 1995; McCrae & Costa, 1991; McAdams, 2009; Magnus et al., 1993). In contrast, the remaining traits, in general, appear to confer an adaptive advantage in relation to stress, health and well-being. For example, extraversion and conscientiousness are associated with positive primary and secondary appraisal and/or adaptive forms of problem-focused coping. In addition, research suggests that the combination of high neuroticism with low extraversion and/or low conscientiousness is associated with stress vulnerability, while the combination of low neuroticism with high extraversion and/or high conscientiousness is associated with stress resistance.

The aim of personality-illness research is to (a) identify the traits (or personality types) that confer risk, (b) to elucidate the mechanisms underlying vulnerability, and (c) to develop intervention strategies for preventing or managing illness and disease (Smith & MacKenzie, 2006). Research on personality and illness is particularly relevant to prevention and the early diagnosis of those at risk, given that traits can serve as a visible marker of underlying or emerging pathology (Suls & Rittenhouse, 1990).

Suls and Martin (2005) described the relationship between neuroticism and stressor exposure, reactivity, cognitive appraisal, and coping as 'neurotic cascade' of reinforcing factors: people who score high on neuroticism report more major life events and daily hassles, show exaggerated affective reactivity to these stressors, appraise or perceive potential stressors as more threatening, and choose maladaptive coping strategies or use coping strategies ineffectively, making recovery from a negative mood more difficult. Maladaptive coping efforts reinforce the neurotic's negative self-concept and sense of helplessness and pessimism, making it more difficult to deal with recurring problems. Interventions to appease the detrimental impact of neuroticism should focus on these multiple processes, in particular: helping neurotics to alter dysfunctional thinking patterns and situational choices that increase stressor exposure; recognize potential positive outcomes when interpreting events rather than focusing negative information; increase their problem-solving self-efficacy; expand their coping skills, including choosing and persisting in the use of adaptive coping strategies; and develop long-term strategies for managing anxiety and negative emotionality. With regard to PDs, generic behavioral interventions could be targeted at those with high neuroticism and low agreeableness, whereas specialized behavioral interventions may be required for extraversion- and conscientiousness-related PDs (Saulsman & Page, 2004). Prevention strategies should utilize scores on neuroticism as a screening tool for physical and mental health problems, to identify early those who are likely to benefit from treatment.

The evidence reviewed above indicates that neuroticism is a consistent risk factor for a range of negative health and well-being outcomes. Although several explanatory mechanisms have been identified in the literature, few studies have evaluated these mechanisms directly, prompting a call for future studies to address this problem (Smith & McKenzie, 2006). Given that neuroticism is associated with a range of conditions, it is likely that the underlying mechanisms are heterogeneous (Goodwin et al., 2006). These mechanisms may include biochemical or psychophysiological pathways beyond the stress process (Goodwin et al., 2006; Smith, 2006). For example, consistent with a direct effect or 'top-down' or dispositional model, both neuroticism and well-being measures show strong correlations over time and strong genetic components in twin studies (Bouchard & Loehlin, 2001; Jang, Livesley, & Vernon, 1996; Lykken & Tellegen, 1996; Nes, Roysamb, Tambs, Harris, & Reichborn-Kjennerud, 2006; Weiss, Bates, & Luciano, 2008), suggesting an underlying genotype. Mechanisms underlying comorbid physical and mental health disorders also need to be explored. A further issue is the direction of causality: ill health or its treatment may increase neuroticism, due to factors such as discomfort/pain or functional limitations associated with illness (Goodwin et al., 2006; Charles, et al., 2008). Equally plausible is a positive or reinforcing feedback loop between negative emotionality and physical ill health. As Smith (2006, p. 230), noted "the elucidation of mechanisms will be important not only for the advance of basic science and its translation into risk reducing intervention; the issue of mechanisms is also important for the credibility of the general perspective that personality can influence health".

REFERENCES

Ahmad, S., James, J., & Ahmad, S. (1991). Organizational role stress: A psychological study of middle managers. *Journal of Personality and Clinical Studies*, *7*, 43-48.

Amirkhan, J. H., Risinger, R. T., & Swickert, R. J. (1995). Extraversion: A "hidden" personality factor in coping. *Journal of Personality*, *63*, 189-212.

Andreassi, J. K. (2007). The role of personality and coping in work-family conflict: New directions. *Dissertation Abstracts International Section A: Humanities and Social Sciences*, *67 (8-A)*, 3053.

Bardi, A., & Ryff, C. D. (2007). Interactive effects of traits on adjustment to a life transition. *Journal of Personality*, *75*, 955-983.

Begley, T. M. (1998). Coping strategies as predictors of employee distress and turnover after an organizational consolidation: A longitudinal analysis. *Journal of Occupational and Organizational Psychology*, *71*, 305-329.

Bluen, S. D., Barling, J., & Burns, W. (1990). Predicting sales performance, job satisfaction, and depression by using the achievement strivings and impatience irritability dimensions of Type A behavior. *Journal of Applied Psychology*, *75*, 212-216.

Bolger, N., & Schilling, E. A. (1991). Personality and the problems of everyday life: The role of neuroticism in exposure and reactivity to daily stressors. *Journal of Personality*, *59*, 355-386.

Bolger, N., & Zuckerman, A. (1995). A framework for studying personality in the stress process. *Journal of Personality and Social Psychology*, *69*, 890-902.

Booth-Kewley, S., & Vickers, R. R. (1994). Associations between major domains of personality and health behavior. *Journal of Personality*, *62*, 281-298.

Bouchard, G. (2003). Cognitive appraisals, neuroticism, and openness as correlates of coping strategies: An integrative model of adaptation to marital difficulties. *Canadian Journal of Behavioral Science*, *35*, 1-12.

Bouchard, T. J., Jr., & Loehlin, J. C. (2001). Genes, evolution, and personality. *Behavior Genetics*, *31*, 243–273.

Bowman, G. D., & Stern, M. (1995). Adjustment to occupational stress: The relationship of perceived control to effectiveness of coping strategies. *Journal of Counseling Psychology*, *42*, 294-303.

Brantley, P. J., & Garrett, D. (1993). Psychobiological approaches to health and disease. In P. B. Sutker & H. E. Adams (Eds.), *Comprehensive handbook of psychopathology (2nd ed.)* (pp. 647-670). New York: Plenum Press.

Brow, M. M. (2008). The role of personality following the September 11th terrorist attacks: Big five trait combinations and interactions in explaining distress and coping. *Dissertation Abstracts International Section B: The Sciences and Engineering*, *69 (5-B)*, 3310.

Brown, D. (1993). Stress and emotion: Implications for illness development and wellness. In S. L. Albion, D. Brown, E. J. Khantzian & J. E. Mack (Eds.), *Human feelings: Explorations in affect development and meaning* (pp. 281-301). Hillside, NJ: Analytic Press.

Callan, V. J., Terry, D. J., & Schweitzer, R. (1994). Coping resources, coping strategies and adjustment to organizational change: Direct or buffering effects? *Work and Stress*, *8*, 372-383.

Carver, C. S., & Scheier, M. F. (1994). Situational coping and coping dispositions in a stressful transaction. *Journal of Personality and Social Psychology*, *66*, 184-195.

Carver, C. S., Scheier, M. F., & Weintraub, J. K. (1989). Assessing coping strategies: A theoretically based approach. *Journal of Personality and Social Psychology*, *56*, 267-283.

Charles, S. T., Gatz, M., Kato, K., & Pedersen, N. L. (2008). Physical health 25 years later: The predictive ability of neuroticism. *Health Psychology*, *27*, 369-378.

Chida, Y., & Hamer, M. (2008). Chronic psychosocial factors and acute physiological responses to laboratory-induced stress in healthy populations: A quantitative review of 30 years of investigations. *Psychological Bulletin*, *134*, 829-885.

Chung, M. C., Berger, Z., Jones, R., & Rudd, H. (2006). Posttraumatic stress disorder and general health problems following myocardial infarction among older patients: The role of personality. *Journal of Geriatric Psychiatry*, *21*, 1163-1174.

Clark, L., Watson, D., & Mineka, S. (1994). Temperament, personality, and the mood and anxiety disorders. *Journal of Abnormal Psychology*, *103*, 103-116.

Cohen, S., & Edwards, J. R. (1989). Personality characteristics as moderators of the relationship between stress and disorder. In R. W. J. Neufeld (Ed.), *Advances in the investigation of psychological stress* (pp. 235-283). New York: Wiley.

Cohen, S., Kamarck, T., & Mermelstein, R. (1983). A global measure of perceived stress. *Journal of Health and Social Behavior*, *24*, 385-396.

Connor-Smith, J. K., & Flachsbart, C. (2007). Relations between personality and coping: A meta-analysis. *Journal of Personality and Social Psychology*, *93*, 1080-1107.

Conard, M. A., & Matthews, R. A. (2008). Modeling the stress process: Personality eclipses dysfunctional cognitions and workload in predicting stress. *Personality and Individual Differences*, *44*, 171-181.

Cook, S. W., & Heppner, P. (1997). A psychometric study of three coping measures. *Educational and Psychological Measurement*, *57*, 906-923.

Costa, P. T., & McCrae, R. R. (1985). *The NEO Personality Inventory Manual.* Odessa, FL: Psychological Assessment Resources.

Costa, P., & McCrae, R. (1990). Personality disorders and the five-factor model of personality. *Journal of Personality Disorders*, *4*, 362-371.

Costa, P. T., & McCrae, R. R. (1992). *Revised NEO Personality Inventory and NEO Five-Factor Inventory: Professional manual.* Odessa, FL: Psychological Assessment Resources.

Costa, P. T., Stone, S. V., McCrae, R. R., Dembroski, T., & Williams, R. B. (1987). Hostility, agreeableness-antagonism and coronary heart disease. *Holistic Medicine*, *2*, 161-167.

Cox, T., & Ferguson, E. (1991). Individual differences, stress and coping. In C. L. Cooper & R. Payne (Eds.), *Personality and stress: Individual differences in the stress process* (pp. 7-30). New York: Wiley.

David, J., Green, P., Martin, R., & Suls, J. (1997). Differential roles of neuroticism, extraversion, and event desirability for mood in daily life: An integrative model of top-down and bottom-up influences. *Journal of Personality and Social Psychology*, *73*, 149-159.

Deary, I. J., Blenkin, H., Agius, R. M., Endler, N. S., Zealley, H., & Wood, R. (1996). Models of job-related stress and achievement among consultant doctors. *British Journal of Psychology*, *87*, 3-29.

Deci, E. L., & Ryan, R. M. (2006). Hedonia, eudaimonia, and well-being: an introduction. *Journal of Happiness Studies*, *9*, 1-11.

de Graaf, R., Bijl, R., Ravelli, A., Smit, F., & Vollenbergh, W. (2002). Predictors of first incidence of DSM-III-R psychiatric disorders in the general population: Findings from the Netherlands Mental Health Survey and Incidence Study. *Acta Psychiatrica Scandinavica*, *106*, 303-313.

Dembroski, T. M. (1985). Components of Type A, hostility, and anger-in: Relationship to angiographic findings. *Psychosomatic Medicine*, *47*, 219-233.

Dembroski, T. M., & Costa, P. T. (1987). Coronary prone behavior: Components of the Type A pattern and hostility. *Journal of Personality*, *55*, 211-235.

Dembroski, T. M., & Costa, P. T. (1988). Assessment of coronary-prone behavior: A current overview. *Annals of Behavioral Medicine*, *10*, 60-63.

DeNeve, K. M., & Cooper, H. (1998). The happy personality: A meta-analysis of 137 personality traits and subjective well-being. *Psychological Bulletin*, *124*, 197-229.

Denollet, J. (1997). Personality, emotional distress and coronary heart disease. *European Journal of Personality*, *11*, 343-357.

Dewe, P., Cox, T., & Ferguson, E. (1993). Individual strategies for coping with stress at work: A review. *Work and Stress*, *7*, 5-15.

Diener, E. (1984). Subjective well-being. *Psychological Bulletin*, *95*, 542-575.

Diener, E., Oishi, S., & Lucas, R. (2003). Personality, culture, and subjective well-being: Emotional and cognitive evaluations of life. *Annual Review of Psychology*, *54*, 403-425.

Digman, J. M. (1990). Personality structure: Emergence of the five-factor model. *Annual Review of Psychology*, *41*, 417-440.

Duru, E., & Poyrazli, S. (2007). Personality dimensions, psychosocial demographic variables, and English language competency in predicting level of acculturative stress among Turkish international students. *International Journal of Stress Management*, *14*, 99-110.

Elliot, A. J., & Sheldon, K. M. (1997). Avoidance achievement motivation: A personal goals analysis. *Journal of Personality and Social Psychology*, *73*, 171-185.

Emmons, R. A., & King, L. A. (1988). Conflict among personal strivings: Immediate and long-term implications for psychological and physical well-being. *Journal of Personality and Social Psychology*, *54*, 1040-1048.

Endler, N. S. (1997). Stress, anxiety and coping: The multidimensional interaction model. *Canadian Psychology*, *38*, 136-153.

Endler, N. S., & Parker, J. D. A. (1994). Assessment of multidimensional coping: Task, emotion, and avoidance coping strategies. *Psychological Assessment*, *6*, 50-60.

Fergusson, D. M., & Horwood, L. J. (1987). Vulnerability to life events exposure. *Psychological Medicine*, *17*, 739-749.

Fickova, E. (2001). Personality regulators of coping behavior in adolescents. *Studia Psychologia*, *43*, 321-329.

Fleming, R., Baum, A., & Singer, J. E. (1984). Toward an integrative approach to the study of stress. *Journal of Personality and Social Psychology*, *46*, 939-949.

Folkman, S., & Lazarus, R. S. (1980). An analysis of coping in a middle-aged community sample. *Journal of Health and Social Behavior*, *21*, 219-239.

Forsythe, C. J., & Compas, B. E. (1987). Interaction of cognitive appraisals of stressful events and coping: Testing the goodness of fit hypothesis. *Cognitive Therapy and Research*, *11*, 473-485.

Friedman, H. S. (1990). Personality and disease: Overview, review and preview. In H. S. Friedman (Ed.), *Personality and disease* (pp. 3-13). New York: Wiley.

Friedman, H. S. (2000). Long-term relations of personality and health: dynamisms, mechanisms and trophisms. *Journal of Personality*, *68*, 1089-1107.

Friedman, H. S., & Booth-Kewley, S. (1987). The "disease prone personality": A meta-analytic view of the construct. *American Psychologist*, *42*, 539-555.

Friedman, M., & Rosenman, R. (1959). Association of specific overt behavior pattern with blood and cardiovascular findings: Blood cholesterol level, blood clotting time, incidence of arcus senilis and clinical coronary artery disease. *Journal of the American Medical Association*, *169*, 1286-1296.

Frokjaer, V. G., Mortensen, E. L., Nielsen, F. A., Haugbol, S., Pinborg, L. H., Adams, K. H., Svarer, C., Hasselbalch, S. G., Steen, G., Holm, S., Paulson, O. B., & Knudson, G. M. (2008). Frontolimbic serotonin 2A receptor binding in healthy subjects is associated with personality risk factors for affective disorder. *Biological Psychiatry*, *63*, 569-576.

Gallagher, D. J. (1990). Extraversion, neuroticism and appraisal of stressful academic events. *Personality and Individual Differences*, *11*, 1053-1057.

Gallant, M. P., & Connell, C. M. (2003). Neuroticism and depressive symptoms among spouse caregivers: Do health behaviors mediate this relationship? *Psychology and Aging*, *18*, 587-592.

Ganster, D. C., Schaubroeck, J., Sime, W. E., & Mayes, B. T. (1991). The nomological validity of the Type A personality among employed adults. *Journal of Applied Psychology*, *76*, 143-168.

Glidden, L. M., Billings, F. J., & Jobe, B. M. (2006). Personality, coping style and well-being of parents rearing children with development disabilities. *Journal of Intellectual Disability Research*, *50*, 949-962.

Goldberg, L. R. (1993). The structure of phenotypic personality traits. *American Psychologist*, *48*, 26-34.

Goodwin, R. D., Cox, B. J., & Clara, I. (2006). Neuroticism and physical disorders among adults in the community: Results from the National Comorbidity Survey. *Journal of Behavioral Medicine*, *29*, 229-238.

Goodwin, R., & Engstrom, G. (2002). Personality and the perception of health in the general population. *Psychological Medicine*, *32*, 325-332.

Goodwin, R. D., & Friedman, H. S. (2006). Health status and the five-factor personality traits in a nationally representative sample. *Journal of Health Psychology*, *11*, 643-654.

Grant, S. L., & Langan-Fox, J. (2006). Occupational stress, coping and strain: the combined/interactive effect of the Big Five traits. *Personality and Individual Differences*, *41*, 719-732.

Grant, S. L., & Langan-Fox, J. (2007). Personality and the occupational stressor-strain relationship: the role of the Big Five. *Journal of Occupational Health Psychology*, *12*, 20-33.

Grant, S. L., Langan-Fox, J., & Anglim, J. (under review). The Big Five traits as predictors of subjective and psychological well-being. *Psychological Reports*.

Gunthert, K. C., Armeli, S., & Cohen, L. H. (1999). The role of neuroticism in daily stress and coping. *Journal of Personality and Social Psychology*, *77*, 1087-1100.

Hellmuth, J. C., & McNulty, J. K. (2008). Neuroticism, marital violence, and the moderating role of stress and behavioral skills. *Journal of Personality and Social Psychology*, *95*, 166-180.

Hemenover, S. H. (2001). Self-reported processing bias and naturally occurring mood: Mediators between personality and stress appraisals. *Personality and Social Psychology Bulletin*, *27*, 387-394.

Hemenover, S. H., & Dienstbier, R. A. (1996). Prediction of stress appraisals from mastery, extraversion, neuroticism, and general appraisal tendencies. *Motivation and Emotion*, *20*, 299-317.

Hills, P., & Argyle, M. (2001). Emotional stability as a major dimension of happiness. *Personality and Individual Differences*, *31*, 1357-1364.

Hirschfeld, R., Klerman, G., Lavori, P., & Keller, M. (1989). Premorbid personality assessments of first onset of major depression. *Archives of General Psychiatry*, *46*, 345-350.

Hobfoll, S. (1988). *The ecology of stress*. New York: Hemisphere.

Holahan, C. K., & Suzuki, R. (2004). Adulthood predictors of health promoting behavior in later aging. *International Journal of Aging and Human Development*, *58*, 289-313.

Holmes, T. H., & Rahe, R. H. (1967). The Social Readjustment Rating Scale. *Journal of Psychosomatic Research*, *11*, 213-218.

Hooker, K., Frazier, L. D., & Monahan, D. J. (1994). Personality and coping among caregivers of spouses with dementia. *The Gerontologist*, *34*, 382-392.

Ingledew, D. K., Hardy, L., Cooper, C. L., & Jemal, H. (1996). Health behaviors reported as coping strategies: A factor analytic study. *British Journal of Health Psychology*, *1*, 263-281.

Ironson, G. H., O'Cleirigh, C., Weiss, A., Schneiderman, N., & Costa, P. T. Jr. (2008). Personality and HIV disease progression: Role of NEO-PI-R openness, extraversion and profiles of engagement. *Psychosomatic Medicine*, *70*, 245-253.

Jang, K., Livesley, W., & Vernon, P. (1996). Heritability of the big five personality dimensions and their facets: A twin study. *Journal of Personality*, *64*, 577-591.

Järvikoski, A., & Härkäpää, K. (1987). A brief Type-A scale and the occurrence of cardiovascular symptoms. *Scandinavian Journal of Rehabilitation Medicine*, *19*, 115-120.

Jerram, K. L., & Coleman, P. G. (1999). The Big Five personality traits and reporting of health problems and health behavior in old age. *British Journal of Health Psychology*, *4*, 181-192.

Jex, S. M. (1998). Stress and job performance: Theory, research and implications for managerial practice. Sage: Thousand Oaks.

Johnson, M. (2003). The vulnerability status of neuroticism: Over-reporting or genuine complaints? *Personality and Individual Differences*, *35*, 877-887.

Karney, B., & Bradbury, T. (1995). The longitudinal course of marital quality and stability: A review of theory, methods, and research. *Psychological Bulletin, 118*, 3-34.

Keyes, C. L. M., Shmotkin, D., & Ryff, C. D. (2002). Optimizing well-being: the empirical encounter of two traditions. *Journal of Personality and Social Psychology, 82*, 1007-1022.

King, A., Bernardy, N., & Hauner, K. (2003). Stressful events, personality, and mood disturbance: Gender differences in alcoholics and problem drinkers. *Addictive Behaviors, 28*, 171-187.

Korotkov, D. (2008). Does personality moderate the relationship between stress and health behavior? Expanding the nomological network of the five-factor model. *Journal of Research in Personality, 42*, 1418-1426.

Korotkov, D., & Hannah, T. E. (2004). The five-factor model of personality: Strengths and limitations in predicting health status, sick-role, and illness behavior. *Personality and Individual Differences, 36*, 187-199.

Kraemer, C. H., Stice, E., Kazdin, A., Offord, D., & Kupfer, D. (2001). How do risk factors work together? Mediators, moderators, and independent, overlapping, and proxy risk factors. *American Journal of Psychiatry, 158*, 848-856.

Kuppens, P., & Van Mechelen, I. (2007). Interactional appraisal models for the anger appraisals of threatened self-esteem, other-blame, and frustration. *Cognition and Emotion, 21*, 56-77.

Kuppens, P., Van Mechelen, I., Smits, D. J. M., De Boeck, P., & Ceulemans, E. (2007). Individual differences in patterns of appraisal and anger experience. *Cognition and Emotion, 21*, 689-713.

Lau, B., Hem, E., Berg, A., Ekeberg, O., & Torgersen, S. (2006). Personality types, coping, and stress in the Norwegian police service. *Personality and Individual Differences, 41*, 971-982.

Lazarus, R. S. (1990). Stress, coping, and illness. In H. S. Friedman (Ed.), *Personality and disease*. New York: Wiley.

Lazarus, R. S., & Folkman, S. (1984). *Stress, appraisal and coping*. New York: Springer-Verlag.

Lee, C. (1992). The relations of personality and cognitive style with job and class performance. *Journal of Organizational Behavior, 13*, 175-185.

Lee, C., Ashford, S. J., & Jamieson, L. F. (1993). The effects of Type A behavior dimensions and optimism on coping strategies, health, and performance. *Journal of Organizational Behavior, 14*, 143-157.

Lemos-Giráldez, S., & Fidalgo-Aliste, A. M. (1997). Personality dispositions and health-related habits and attitudes: A cross-sectional study. *European Journal of Personality*, *11*, 197-209.

Lepore, S. J. (1995). Measurement of chronic stressors. In S. Cohen, R. C. Kessler & L. Underwood-Gordon (Eds.), *Measuring stress: A guide for health and social scientists* (pp. 102-120). New York: Oxford University Press.

Leventhal, H., & Tomarken, A. (1987). Stress and illness: Perspectives from health psychology. In S. V. Kasl & C. L. Cooper (Eds.), *Stress and health: Issues in research methodology._Wiley series on studies in occupational stress* (pp. 27-55). Oxford, England: Wiley.

Long, B. (1993). Coping strategies of male managers: A prospective analysis of predictors of psychosomatic symptoms and job satisfaction. *Journal of Vocational Behavior*, *42*, 184-199.

Lucas, R., Diener, E., & Suh, E. (1996). Discriminant validity of well-being measures. *Journal of Personality and Social Psychology*, *71*, 616-628.

Lykken, D. T., & Tellegen, A. (1996). Happiness is a stochastic phenomenon. *Psychological Science*, *7*, 186–189.

MacDougall, J. M., Dembroski, T. M., Dimsdale, J. E., & Hackett, T. P. (1985). Components of Type A, hostility, and anger-in: Further relationships to angiographic findings. *Health Psychology*, *4*, 137-152.

Magnus, K., Diener, E., Fujita, F., & Payot, W. (1993). Extraversion and neuroticism as predictors of objective life events: A longitudinal analysis. *Journal of Personality and Social Psychology*, *65*, 1046-1053.

Mäkikangas, A., & Kinnunen, U. (2003). Psychosocial work stressors and well-being: Self-esteem and optimism as moderators in a one-year longitudinal sample. *Personality and Individual Differences*, *35*, 537-557.

Malyszczak, K., Pyszel, A., Lindner, K., Wrobel, T., Mazur, G., Kiejna, A., Kuliczkowski, K., & Andrzejak, R. (2007). General psychological distress and personality traits in physically ill patients. *Archives of Psychiatry and Psychotherapy*, *9*, 57-60.

Mangold, D. L., Veraza, R., Kinker, L., & Kinney, N. A. (2007). Neuroticism predicts acculturative stress in Mexican American college students. *Hispanic Journal of Behavioral Sciences*, *29*, 366-382.

Mangold, D. L., & Wand, G. S. (2006). Cortisol and andrenocorticotropic hormone responses to naloxone in subjective with high and low neuroticism. *Biological Psychiatry*, *60*, 850-855.

Marco, C., & Suls, J. (1993). Daily stress and the trajectory of mood: Spillover, response assimilation, contrast, and chronic negative affectivity. *Journal of Personality and Social Psychology*, *64*, 1053-1063.

Markey, C. N., Markey, P. M., Ericksen, A. J., & Tinsley, B. J. (2006). Children's behavioral patterns, the Five Factor model of personality, and risk behaviors. *Personality and Individual Differences*, *41*, 1503-1513.

Matheny, K. B., Aycock, D. W., Curlette, W. L., & Junker, G. N. (1993). The Coping Resources Inventory for Stress: A measure of perceived resourcefulness. *Journal of Clinical Psychology*, *49*, 815-830.

Matthews, G., Emo, A. K., Funke, G., Zeidner, M., Roberts, R. D., Costa, P. T. Jr., & Schulze, R. (2006). Emotional intelligence, personality and task induced stress. *Journal of Experimental Psychology: Applied*, *12*, 96-107.

Maxim, L. A. (2000). Cognitive mediation of coping: A prospective, longitudinal study. *Dissertation Abstracts International: Section B: The Sciences and Engineering*, *61(4-B)*, 2210.

McAdams, D. P. (2009). The person: An introduction to the science of personality psychology (5th ed.). Hoboken, NJ: Wiley.

McClelland, D. C. (1985). The social mandate of health psychology. *American Behavioral Scientist*, *28*, 451-467.

McCrae, R., & Costa, P. (1986). Personality, coping, and coping effectiveness in an adult sample. *Journal of Personality*, *54*, 385-405.

McCrae, R. R., & Costa, P. T. (1987). Validation of the five-factor model of personality across instruments and observers. *Journal of Personality and Social Psychology*, *52*, 81-90.

McCrae, R. R., & Costa, P. T. (1991). Adding liebe und arbeit: the full five-factor model and well-being. *Personality and Social Psychology Bulletin*, *17*, 227-232.

McCrae, R. R., Costa, P. T., & Busch, C. M. (1986). Evaluating comprehensiveness in personality systems: The California Q Set and the five-factor model. *Journal of Personality*, *54*, 430-446.

McCrae, R. R., & John, O. P. (1992). An introduction to the five-factor model and its applications. *Journal of Personality*, *60*, 175-215.

Michaels, C., Michaels, A., & Peterson, C. (1997). Motivation and health. *Advances in Motivation and Achievement*, *10*, 339-374.

Monroe, S. M., & Kelley, J. M. (1997). Measurement of stress appraisal. In S. Cohen, R. C. Kessler & L. Underwood-Gordon (Eds.), *Measuring stress: A guide for health and social scientists* (pp. 122-147). New York: Oxford University Press.

Moor, C., Zimprich, D., Schmitt, M., & Kliegel, M. (2006). Personality, aging self-perceptions, and subjective health: A mediation model. *International Journal of Aging and Human Development*, *63*, 241-257.

Nes, R. B., Roysamb, E., Tambs, K., Harris, J. R., & Reichborn-Kjennerud, T. (2006). Subjective well-being: genetic and environmental contributions to stability and change. *Psychological Medicine*, *36*, 1033–1042.

Newton, T. J., & Keenan, T. (1990). The moderating effect of the Type A behavior pattern and locus of control upon the relationship between change in job demands and change in psychological strain. *Human Relations*, *43*, 1229-1255.

O'Brien, T. B., & DeLongis, A. (1996). The interactional context of problem-, emotion-, and relationship-focused coping: The role of the Big Five personality factors. *Journal of Personality*, *64*, 775-813.

Ormel, J., & Wohlfarth, T. (1991). How neuroticism, long-term difficulties, and life situation change influence psychological distress: A longitudinal model. *Journal of Personality and Social Psychology*, *60*, 744-755.

Parasuraman, S., & Cleek, M. A. (1984). Coping behaviors and managers' affective reactions to role stressors. *Journal of Vocational Behavior*, *24*, 179-193.

Parkes, K. R. (1994). Personality and coping as moderators of work stress processes: Models, methods and measures. *Work and Stress*, *8*, 110-129.

Payne, R. (1991). Individual differences in cognition and the stress process. In C. L. Cooper & R. Payne (Eds.), *Personality and stress: Individual differences in the stress process* (pp. 181-201). New York: Wiley.

Peacock, E. J., & Wong, P. T. P. (1990). The Stress Appraisal Measure (SAM): A multidimensional approach to cognitive appraisal. *Stress Medicine*, *6*, 227-236.

Peltzer, K. (2004). Preventive health behavior, personality and religiosity among black and white South Africans. *Studia Psychologica*, *46*, 37-48.

Penley, J. A., & Tomaka, J. (2002). Associations among the Big Five, emotional responses, and coping with acute stress. *Personality and Individual Differences*, *32*, 1215-1228.

Phillips, A., Carroll, D., Burns, V., & Drayson, M. (2005). Neuroticism, cortisol reactivity, and antibody response to vaccination. *Psychophysiology*, *42*, 232-238.

Poulton, R., & Andrews, G. (1992). Personality as a cause of adverse life events. *Acta Psychiatrica Scandinavica*, *85*, 35-38.

Powell, L. H. (1987). Issues in the measurement of the Type A behavior pattern. In S. V. Kasl & C. L. Cooper (Eds.), *Stress and health: Issues in research methodology. Wiley series on studies in occupational stress* (pp. 231-281). Oxford, England: Wiley.

Revenson, T. A. (1990). All other things are not equal: An ecological approach to personality and disease. In H. S. Friedman (Ed.), *Personality and disease* (pp. 65-94). New York: Wiley.

Riese, H., Harriate, R., Rosmalen, J. G. M., Ormel, J., Van Roon, A. Oldehinkel, A J., & Rijsdijk, F. V. (2007). The genetic relationship between neuroticism and autonomic function in female twins. *Psychological Medicine, 37*, 257-267.

Rovik, J. O., Tyssen, R., Gude, T., Moum, T., Ekeberg, O., & Vaglum, P. (2007). Exploring the interplay between personality dimensions: A comparison of the typological and the dimensional approach in stress research. *Personality and Individual Differences, 42*, 1255-1266.

Rust, J. (1999). Discriminant validity of the "Big Five" personality traits in employment settings. *Social Behavior and Personality, 27*, 99-108.

Ryan, R. M., & Deci, E. L. (2001). On happiness and human potentials: A review of research on hedonic and eudaimonic well-being. *Annual Review of Psychology, 52*, 141-166.

Ryff, C. D. (1989). Happiness is everything, or is it? Explorations on the meaning of psychological well-being. *Journal of Personality and Social Psychology, 57*, 1069-1081.

Ryff, C., & Singer, B. (1996). Psychological well-being: Meaning, measurement, and implications for psychotherapy research. *Psychotherapy and Psychosomatics, 65*, 14-23.

Samuel, D. B., & Widiger, T. A. (2008). A meta-analtyic review of the relationship between the five-factor model and DSM-IV-TR personality disorders: A facet level analysis. *Clinical Psychology Review, 28*, 1326-1342.

Saulsman, L. M., & Page, A. C. (2004). The five-factor model and personality disorder empirical literature: A meta-analytic review. *Clinical Psychology Review, 23*, 1055-1085.

Schmutte, P. S., & Ryff, C. D. (1997). Personality and well-being: re-examining methods and meanings. *Journal of Personality and Social Psychology, 73*, 549-559.

Semmer, N. (1996). Individual differences, work stress and health. In M. J. Schabracq, J. A. M. Winnubst & C. L. Cooper (Eds.), *Handbook of work and health psychology* (pp. 51-86). New York: Wiley.

Shewchuk, R. M., Elliott, T. R., MacNair-Semands, R. R., & Harkins, S. (1999). Trait influences on stress appraisal and coping: An evaluation of alternative frameworks. *Journal of Applied Social Psychology*, *29*, 685-704.

Shipley, B. A., Weiss, A., Der, G., Taylor, M. D., & Deary, I. J. (2008). Neuroticism, extraversion, and mortality in the UK Health and Lifestyle Survey: A 21-year prospective cohort study. *Psychosomatic Medicine*, *69*, 923-931.

Siegall, M., & Cummings, L. L. (1995). Stress and organizational role conflict. *Genetic, Social, and General Psychology Monographs*, *121*, 65-95.

Siegler, I. C., & Brummet, B. H. (2000). and well-being at midlife: facet-level analyses. *Psychology and Aging*, *15*, 710-714.

Siegrist, J. (1995). Emotions and health in occupational life: New scientific findings and policy implications. *Patient Education and Counseling*, *25*, 227-236.

Siegrist, J. (2003). Subjective well-being: new conceptual and methodological developments in health-related social sciences. *ESF SCSS Exploratory Workshop on Income, Interactions and Subjective Well-being*. Paris, 25-26 September.

Smillie, L., Pickering, A., & Jackson, C. (2006). The new reinforcement sensitivity theory: implications for personality measurement. *Personality and Social Psychology Review*, *10*, 320-335.

Smith, T. W. (2006). Personality as risk and resilience in physical health. *Current Directions in Psychological Science*, *15*, 227-231.

Smith, T. W., & MacKenzie, J. (2006). Personality and risk of physical illness. *Annual Review of Clinical Psychology*, *2*, 435-467.

Spector, P. E., & O'Connell, B. J. (1994). The contribution of personality traits, negative affectivity, locus of control and Type A to subsequent reports of job stressors and job strains. *Journal of Occupational and Organizational Psychology*, *67*, 1-11.

Spence, J. T., Helmreich, R. L., Pred, R. S. (1987). Impatience versus achievement strivings in the Type A pattern: Differential effects on students' health and academic achievement. *Journal of Applied Psychology*, *72*, 522-528.

Spence, J. T., Pred, R. S., & Helmreich, R. L. (1989). Achievement strivings, scholastic aptitude, and academic performance: A follow up to "Impatience versus achievement strivings in the Type A pattern." *Journal of Applied Psychology*, *74*, 176-178.

Steel, P., Schmidt, J., & Shultz, J. (2008). Refining the relationship between personality and subjective well-being. *Psychological Bulletin, 134*, 138-161.

Stone, S. V., & Costa, P. T. Jr. (1990). Disease prone personality or distress prone personality? The role of neuroticism in coronary heart disease. In H. S. Friedman (Ed.), *Personality and disease* (pp. 178-200). New York: Wiley.

Suls, J., Green, P., & Hillis, S. (1998). Emotional reactivity to everyday problems, affective inertia, and neuroticism. *Personality and Social Psychology Bulletin*, *24*, 127-136.

Suls, J., & Martin, R. (2005). The daily life of the garden variety neurotic: reactivity, stressor exposure, mood spillover, and maladaptive coping. *Journal of Personality, Special Issue: Advances in Personality and Daily Experience*, *73*, 1485-1510.

Suls, J., Martin, R., & David, J. (1998). Person-environment fit and its limits: Agreeableness, neuroticism, and emotional reactivity to interpersonal conflict. *Personality and Social Psychology Bulletin*, *24*, 88-98.

Suls, J., & Rittenhouse, J. D. (1987). Personality and physical health: An introduction. *Journal of Personality*, *55*, 155-167.

Suls, J., & Rittenhouse, J. D. (1990). Models of linkages between personality and disease. In H. S. Friedman (Ed.), *Personality and disease* (pp. 38-64). New York: Wiley.

Tomaka, J., Blascovich, J., Kesley, R. M., & Leitten, C. L. (1993). Subjective, physiological and behavioral effects of threat and challenge appraisal. *Journal of Personality and Social Psychology*, *65*, 248-260.

Tucker, J. S., Elliot, M. N., & Klein, D. J. (2006). Social control of health behavior: Associations with conscientiousness and neuroticism. *Personality and Social Psychology Bulletin*, *32*, 1143-1152.

Tyssen, R., Dolatowski, F. C., Rovik, J. O., Thorkildsen, R. F., Ekeberg, O., Hem, E., Gude, T., Gronvold, N. T., & Vaglum, P. (2007). Personality traits and types predict medical school stress: a six year longitudinal and nationwide study. *Medical Education*, *41*, 781-787.

van Dierendonck, D. (2005). The construct validity of Ryff's Scales of Psychological Well-being and its extension with spiritual well-being. *Personality and Individual Differences*, *36*, 629-643.

Vingerhoets, A. J., Croon, M., Jeninga, A. J., & Menges, L. J., (1990). Personality and health habits. *Psychology and Health*, *4*, 333-342.

Vittersø, J. (2001). Personality traits and subjective well-being: Emotional stability, not extraversion, is probably the important predictor. *Personality and Individual Differences*, *31*, 903-914.

Vollrath, M. (2001). Personality and stress. *Scandinavian Journal of Psychology*, *42*, 335-347.

Vollrath, M., Knoch, D., & Cassano, L. (1999). Personality, risky health behavior, and perceived susceptibility to health risks. *European Journal of Personality, 13*, 39-50.

Vollrath, M., & Torgersen, S. (2000). Personality types and coping. *Personality and Individual Differences, 29*, 367-378.

Vollrath, M., & Torgersen, S. (2002). Who takes health risks? A probe into eight personality types. *Personality and Individual Differences, 32*, 1185-1197.

Vollrath, M. E., & Torgersen, S. (2008). Personality types and risky health behaviors in Norwegian students. *Scandinavian Journal of Psychology, 49*, 287-292.

Vollrath, M., Torgersen, S., & Alnæs, R. (1995). Personality as a long-term predictor of coping. *Personality and Individual Differences, 18*, 117-125.

Ward, C. H., & Eisler, R. M. (1987a). Type A behavior, achievement striving, and a dysfunctional self-evaluation system. *Journal of Personality and Social Psychology, 53*, 318-326.

Ward, C. H., & Eisler, R. M. (1987b). Type A achievement striving and failure to achieve personal goals. *Cognitive Therapy and Research, 11*, 463-471.

Watson, D., & Clark, L. A. (1984). Negative affectivity: The disposition to experience aversive emotional states. *Psychological Bulletin, 96*, 465-490.

Watson, D., Clark, L. A., & Tellegen, A. (1988). Development and validation of brief measures of positive and negative affect: The PANAS scales. *Journal of Personality and Social Psychology, 54*, 1063-1070.

Watson, D., & Hubbard, B. (1996). Adaptational style and dispositional structure: Coping in the context of the five-factor model. *Journal of Personality, 64*, 737-774.

Watson, D., & Pennebaker, J. W. (1989). Health complaints, stress, and distress: Exploring the central role of negative affectivity. *Psychological Review, 96*, 234-254.

Weinstock, L., & Whisman, M. (2006). Neuroticism as a common feature of the depressive and anxiety disorders: A test of the revised integrative hierarchical model in a national sample. *Journal of Abnormal Psychology, 115*, 68-74.

Widiger, T. A., & Lowe, J. R. (2008). A dimensional model of personality disorder: Proposal for DSM-V. *Psychiatric Clinics of North America, 31*, 363-378.

Widiger, T. A., & Samuel, D. B. (2005). Diagnostic categories or dimensions ? A question for the Diagnostic and Statistical Manual of Mental Disorders

– Fifth Edition. *Journal of Abnormal Psychology, Special Issue: Toward a Dimensionality Based Taxonomy of Psychopathology*, *114*, 494-504.

Widiger, T. A., Simonsen, E., Krueger, R. F., Livesley, W. J., & Verheul, R. (2006). Personality disorder research agenda for DSM-V. In T. A. Widiger, E. Simonsen, P. J. Sirovatka, & D. A. Regier (Eds.), *Dimensional models of personality disorders: Refining the research agenda for DSM-V* (pp. 233-256). Washington, DC: American Psychological Association.

Widiger, T. A., & Trull, T. J. (2007). Plate tectonics in the classification of personality disorder: Shifting to a dimensional model. *American Psychologist*, *62*, 71-83.

Wiebe, D. J., & Smith, T. W. (1997). Personality and health: Progress and problems in psychosomatics. In R. Hogan, J. Johnson & S. Briggs (Eds.), *Handbook of personality psychology* (pp. 891–918). San Diego: Academic Press.

Weiss, A., Bates, T. C., & Luciano, M. (2008). Happiness is a personal(ity) thing: the genetics of personality and well-being in a representative sample. *Psychological Science, 19*, 205-210.

Williams, P. G., O'Brien, C. D., & Colder, C. R. (2004). The effects of neuroticism and extraversion on self-assessed health and health-relevant cognition. *Personality and Individual Differences*, *37*, 83-94.

Williams, L., O'Connor, R. C., Howard, S., Hughes, B. M., Johnston, D. W., Hay, J. L., O'Connor, D. B., Lewis, C. A., Ferguson, E., Sheehy, N., Grealy, M. A., & O'Carroll, R. E. (2008). Type-D personality mechanisms of effect: The role of health-related behavior and social support. *Journal of Psychosomatic Research*, *64*, 63-69.

Wilson, R. S., Krueger, K. R., Gu, L., Bienias, J. L., Mendes de Leon, C. F., & Evans, D. A. (2005). Neuroticism, extraversion, and mortality in a defined population of older persons. *Psychosomatic Medicine*, *67*, 841-845.

Winter, D. G. (1996). Personality: Analysis and interpretation of lives. New York: McGraw-Hill.

Zautra, A. J., Affleck, G. G., Tennen, H., Reich, J. W., & Davis, M. C. (2005). Dynamic approaches to emotions and stress in everyday life: Bolger and Zuckerman reloaded with positive as well as negative affects. *Journal of Personality, Special Issue: Advances in Personality and Daily Experience*, *73*, 1511-1538.

Zonderman, A., Herbst, J., Schmidt, C., Costa, P., & McCrae, R. (1993). Depressive symptoms as a nonspecific, graded risk for psychiatric diagnoses. *Journal of Abnormal Psychology*, *102*, 544-552.

INDEX

D

E

F

G

O

P

Q

R

S

T

U

V

W